WOODLAND
MOUNDS
in West Virginia

WOODLAND MOUNDS
in West Virginia

Darla Spencer

THE
History
PRESS

Published by The History Press
Charleston, SC
www.historypress.com

Front cover, top: Grave Creek Mound. *Courtesy of Heather Cline*; *bottom left*: Steatite platform pipe from Mound No. 21, the Great Smith Mound. *Courtesy of Smithsonian Museum Department of Anthropology (Catalogue No. 90840)*; *bottom center*: Reconstructed turtle effigy tablet from Cresap Mound. *Courtesy of the Carnegie Museum of Natural History*; bottom right: Stone effigy bird head from "Ancient City of Kanawha." *Courtesy of the Smithsonian Museum Department of Anthropology (Catalogue No. 90710)*.
Back cover, top: Grave Creek Mound. *From Squier and Davis,* Ancient Monuments of the Mississippi Valley, *1848*; *bottom left*: Stone bird effigy pipe from the Willow Island Mound. *Courtesy of the Grave Creek Mound Archaeological Complex, West Virginia Department of Arts, Culture and History*; *bottom right*: Stone pipe from "Ancient City of Kanawha." *Courtesy of Smithsonian Museum Department of Anthropology (Catalogue No. 90668)*.

First published 2019

Manufactured in the United States

ISBN 9781467138659

Library of Congress Control Number: 2019935366

Notice: The information in this book is true and complete to the best of our knowledge. It is offered without guarantee on the part of the author or The History Press. The author and The History Press disclaim all liability in connection with the use of this book.

This book is dedicated to my sons, Logan and Damon Hoffman.

This project is presented with financial assistance from the West Virginia Humanities Council, a state affiliate of the National Endowment for the Humanities. Any views, findings, conclusions or recommendations do not necessarily represent those of the West Virginia Humanities Council or the National Endowment for the Humanities.

CONTENTS

FOREWORD

I have worked as an archaeologist in West Virginia for twenty-five years, specializing in Native American cultures before the arrival of Europeans. While most of my time has been spent working with other archaeologists, I have also interacted extensively with amateur archaeologists and the general public. An important takeaway for me from these diverse interactions is that many West Virginians, regardless of their background, education or profession, have an interest in knowing more about the ancient native peoples who once inhabited the hills, hollows and valleys of the state and, in particular, those who built and used the mounds and earthworks that were once a common element of the landscape in some of the state's larger river valleys. To this end, it seemed obvious that having a volume that pulled together and clearly summarized the scattered information for these ancient mound-building societies, from which the state's earliest landscape architects emerged, would benefit everyone from the professional archaeologist to the casual reader.

Having such summary works that would be useful to the professional and of interest and value to the public had long been the vison of my longtime friend and former co-worker Darla Spencer. As a native West Virginian, and having been educated in state and also having spent a good part of her career as a professional archaeologist, she was eminently aware of the difficulty many archaeologists and graduate students had in tracking down and acquiring reference materials for their research and, perhaps more importantly, how the general public held many misconceptions regarding the origin and history of the state's native peoples. As the first step in fulfilling her vison, she utilized her considerable energy and talents to research the Late Prehistoric peoples of the state, which culminated in the publication of *Early Native Americans in West Virginia: The Fort Ancient Culture*. This well-received volume, published in 2016, provided an overview of the archaeology and lifeways for a specific period of time and cultural development in the state's past and has become a valuable reference tool for the professional and non-professional alike.

Based on the overwhelming popularity of her 2016 publication, Spencer embarked to further her vision, and in her current work, *Woodland Mounds in West Virginia*, she has gathered information for many of the ancient mounds, and in particular those located in the Kanawha and Ohio River valleys, where the majority of previous research has been conducted. Using the same clear and informative writing style as in her previous volume, she provides a chronologically organized discussion of significant changes in Native American lifeways and culture, providing a context to better understand when and how some of the better-documented mounds in the state were constructed and used. Once the context is set, she describes, often in considerable detail, the excavations of the mounds and the artifacts that were recovered. The accompanying photographs provide a representation of the variety of artifacts placed within the mounds and clearly demonstrate the high level of skill and talent possessed by the ancient artisans of these mound-building societies.

While I'm sure this volume will prove valuable to the professional, student and amateur archaeologist working in the Ohio Valley for the information and references it provides, I believe it will be more widely appreciated by the general public for the information and clarity it provides for the widely misunderstood topic of the "Mound Builders."

MICHAEL ANSLINGER

PREFACE

Invariably, when someone discovers that I am an archaeologist, one of the first questions they ask is about the burial mounds located throughout the state. Sometimes they know of a mound on someone's property that has not been recorded. The conical earthen mounds throughout West Virginia and the Ohio Valley are one of the only visible reminders that native people lived here long before the arrival of the first Europeans. That is one of my reasons for writing this book.

When the first Europeans crossed the Appalachian Mountains and arrived in the Ohio Valley, they were intrigued by the many conical earthen mounds they encountered there. For many years, these structures and their history were a mystery. They were thought to be the remnants of a lost race of people and not the ancestors of the Native Americans who were living in the Ohio Valley at the time. It was not until the 1880s, when the Smithsonian Institution sent investigators to explore the mounds, that this mystery was finally solved, and the ancestors of Native Americans were determined to be the builders of the mounds. This was also the beginning of archaeology in America.

Over four hundred burial mounds have been recorded in West Virginia,[1] but few have been professionally investigated. This volume will present an introduction to what is currently known about the early Native American mound-building cultures of the Woodland period in West Virginia and explore sixteen of the most well-known and better-documented mounds and groups of mounds throughout the state from this time. It is intended to be a reference for archaeologists as well as an introduction to the Woodland period for non-archaeologists.

ACKNOWLEDGEMENTS

Several individuals and organizations helped bring this work to completion. I would like to express my gratitude to the following parties:

The History Press and Kate Jenkins and Hilary Parrish for their help and guidance during the preparation of the book;

Mike Anslinger of Cultural Resource Analysts for preparing the foreword for the book and for reviewing portions of the text;

A special thanks to Jim Kompanek of Cultural Resource Analysts for preparation of the site location map for the book;

The West Virginia Humanities Council for funding my research for the book and for funding archaeological research in West Virginia through the years;

The Smithsonian Institution Department of Anthropology and David Rosenthal and James Krakker for permission to photograph artifacts from their collections from mounds in West Virginia;

The Penn Museum and William Wierzbowski and Eric Schnittke for permission to photograph artifacts from the Beech Bottom Mound and for preparing images for the book;

The Carnegie Museum of Natural History and Deborah Harding and Amy Covell for permission to photograph artifacts from the Cresap Mound collections and for scanning images from the original plates for the book;

The Grave Creek Mound Archaeological Complex and Heather Cline and Hank Lutton for permission to photograph artifacts from the facility's collections. A special thanks to Heather Cline for providing excellent photographs of the Grave Creek Mound;

The William S. Webb Museum of Anthropology and George Crothers for permission to use material from their publications;

The West Virginia Geological and Economic Survey for permission to use material from their publications;

The West Virginia Archeological Society for permission to use material from their publications;

The West Virginia Division of Highways and Ben Hark for permission to use information from the Cotiga Mound report;

And, of course, a special thanks to my family for their support and patience during the past year while my focus was elsewhere.

Chapter 1

BACKGROUND AND ARCHAEOLOGICAL DESIGNATED PERIODS

Historically, the area now known as West Virginia was considered an early Native American "hunting ground" that lacked permanent occupations. But at the same time, evidence for prehistoric occupations in the form of material culture, or artifacts, was plentiful throughout the state, often occurring in dense concentrations and containing the remains of pottery and other artifacts suggestive of intensive domestic activity and, in some cases, sedentary village life. In addition, hundreds of prehistoric burial mounds were visible. Archaeological research conducted during the twentieth century demonstrated that the history of Native American occupation throughout the hills, hollows and valleys of West Virginia was similar to that of adjacent areas, and there was abundant evidence of a continuous Native American presence extending from the end of the last ice age, roughly some fourteen thousand to twelve thousand years ago, to the time of European contact. The long-held myth that West Virginia was only used as a hunting ground by Native Americans was finally put to rest.

ARCHAEOLOGICAL DESIGNATED PERIODS

Our current understanding of the native peoples of West Virginia and surrounding areas is based on archaeological investigations and associated analyses spanning nearly 140 years. Based on the information obtained from these investigations, Native American history in the Ohio Valley has been described as a continuum of culture change that began with the earliest hunter-gatherer groups who entered North America during the waning of the last ice age to the village-dwelling farming communities that were encountered after European contact.[2] Over these millennia, the Native American populations grew and became increasingly regionally diverse as they adapted to changing post–ice age environments and gradually became more sedentary.

In their attempt to interpret and understand the vastly diverse array of archaeological sites and material remains left scattered across the landscape by the many millennia of Native American occupation, archaeologists developed systems for classifying or ordering the archaeological record. The most widely accepted system, and the one widely used today by Ohio Valley archaeologists, categorizes archaeological sites into four broad, successive periods, which, from oldest to youngest, are Paleo-Indian, Archaic, Woodland and Late Prehistoric/ Protohistoric. The periods have been assigned beginning and ending dates based on radiocarbon dates. This ordering of the archaeological record is not arbitrary, with the divisions between periods reflecting changes or shifts in one or more significant aspects of life, whether it be social, economic or technological. Within each period, peoples living in a region generally shared common lifestyles and technologies, and overall, their similarities were greater than their differences. However, the archaeological record does document considerable intra- and interregional variability.

Most of the information that has enabled archaeologists to order the archaeological record and to better understand the changing lifeways of native peoples during the aforementioned periods is in large part the result of the more rigorous or scientific approach to archaeological excavation and analysis, which gained great momentum in North America beginning in the 1960s and 1970s. During this period, excavations were more carefully executed than many had been in the past and were designed to address specific research questions with careful attention given to the context from which artifacts were recovered. At this time, the radiocarbon dating method, which had been developed in the late 1940s, was beginning to be widely used to date sites across the country, allowing archaeologists for the first time to accurately determine the ages of the sites they were investigating. As the number of dated sites grew, it was possible to more accurately order them and their associated characteristics, including artifact types and styles, in time. The dates also provided better evidence for the antiquity of native peoples in North America. For example, by the 1960s, a suite of radiocarbon dates for the St. Albans archaeological site on the Kanawha River near

Charleston, West Virginia, provided evidence of repeated short-term occupations beginning nearly ten thousand years ago.[3]

Also, archaeologists working in the region were becoming increasingly interested in reconstructing the diets of native peoples and gaining a better understanding of the origins of agriculture and the transition from hunter-gatherers to farmers. While the bones and other remains of the animals they hunted were easily identified, recovered and analyzed, the same was not always true for the remains of plants that were consumed given their typically small size and fragile nature. With great success, this obstacle was overcome with the introduction of the flotation method, which consists of the controlled water processing of soil samples collected from sites to recover small bits of charcoal, carbonized seeds and other materials that would otherwise not be recovered. The recovered botanical materials, when examined by specialists, provided information useful for reconstructing the role of plants for different cultural groups through time. The information is also useful for reconstructing past environments. As a result of the use of the flotation method in archaeology, which was widely adopted in the Ohio Valley during the 1970s and is a standard laboratory method used in modern excavations, archaeologists now possess considerable knowledge of the types of wild and cultivated plants consumed/used by native groups and, importantly, the timing of significant changes in their diets, which over the millennia shifted from the use of wild plants acquired by foraging to corn-based agriculture.

The wealth of information obtained by archaeologists and other scientists from field investigations and the analysis of artifacts and other material remains in the laboratory, including radiocarbon dating and the analysis of plant remains discussed above, provides the foundation for the four-period classification system previously discussed. The information available to archaeologists in the Upper Ohio Valley, including West Virginia, is the result of some 140 years of exploration and study, which continues today.

THE PALEO-INDIAN PERIOD
(~13000 BC TO 8000 BC)

There remains considerable debate among archaeologists as to when and how the first peoples arrived in North America and settled the continent. For the Ohio Valley, a starting date of around fifteen thousand years ago, or 13000 BC, is within the generally accepted range of when the first people entered the region. However, there are new discoveries of early Native American occupation in the Americas occurring frequently, and the earliest known dates are subject to change. The first known colonization of North America was by peoples termed Paleo-Indians by archaeologists. The archaeological evidence indicates that Paleo-Indians were highly mobile hunting-gathering peoples who are believed to have followed the large mammals, or megafauna, across the Bering Strait into North America near the end of the last ice age. Early spear or thrusting darts and butchering tools made of high-quality flint, obsidian and other types of stone have been recovered in direct association with extinct mammal species in the Great Plains and other western states. In the eastern part of the country, most evidence for Paleo-Indians is in the form of distinctive spear points found on the surfaces of plowed fields and, less frequently, in undisturbed contexts buried in the valleys of rivers and in rock shelters and caves. During the latter part of the period, Paleo-Indians in the Eastern Woodlands probably hunted migratory herds of caribou.

At the end of the ice age and the beginning of the modern era, which we are in now, the climate warmed and the glaciers retreated. Many of the megafauna were unable to adapt to the changing climate and became extinct. In response, the native people were forced to change their diets to survive. Smaller mammals, such as the elk and the white-tailed deer, became important food sources, and new tools and strategies were developed to hunt them. These changes in technology and lifestyle transitioned into what archaeologists call the Archaic period.

THE ARCHAIC PERIOD (8000 BC TO 1000 BC)

At the beginning of the Archaic period, native people in eastern North America continued to live in small, highly mobile, kin-based groups. They still led a hunter-gatherer lifestyle as before, traveling from area to area to hunt and collect food, although within smaller geographical areas. Over time, regional differences in the styles of spear points developed, suggesting that as they adapted and settled into an area or region, groups were differentiating themselves from adjacent groups and developing their own cultural identities. Such differences are particularly noticeable at the regional scale.

Instead of the large megafauna hunted during the Paleo-Indian period, Archaic peoples hunted animals we see today, such as white-tailed deer and a variety of small mammals, birds and reptiles, and in places, they also took fish and mussels from rivers and streams. During the early part of the period, when groups were more mobile and probably traveled greater distances, they were able to acquire many of the best chert/flint types available, which provided the raw stone from which they manufactured their spear points, knives, scrapers and other tools used to hunt and process game. For example, Vanport (or Flint Ridge) chert from Ohio and Wyandotte chert from Indiana are found in the form of completed and typically used spear points throughout the Ohio Valley and in adjacent areas during the early part of the period. Other types of stone, including locally available sandstone and igneous and metamorphic rock transported into Ohio and Indiana by glaciers, were also widely used to make implements, including woodworking tools such as axes and celts and multipurpose hammerstones and anvils. Later, most groups used raw materials that were local to their area.

In the Upper Ohio Valley, burial mounds have not been dated to the Archaic period, and most burials are found in pits within habitation sites. There is little evidence for mortuary ceremonialism, and most artifacts are utilitarian; non-utilitarian artifacts are rarely discovered. Near the end of the period, native peoples became more sedentary and began to domesticate the first wild plants for food and in some places produce ceramic pottery. These changes in lifestyle led to what archaeologists call the Woodland period.

THE WOODLAND PERIOD (1000 BC TO AD 1000)

Archaeologists traditionally distinguish the Woodland period from the preceding Archaic period by the beginnings of plant domestication, the appearance of ceramic pottery and the construction of burial mounds. However, we now know that each of these developments appeared in parts of the Upper Ohio Valley centuries before 1000 BC. During the Woodland period, the Adena and Hopewell cultural traditions, which were responsible for most of the mounds and earthworks constructed in the Upper Ohio Valley, flourished. These cultural traditions are best expressed in southern Ohio, although their influences permeated adjacent areas, including parts of West Virginia. By the latter part of the period few, if any, mounds were being constructed.

THE LATE PREHISTORIC AND PROTOHISTORIC PERIODS (CIRCA AD 1000 TO AD 1690)

Around AD 1000, the lifestyles of Native Americans throughout the Ohio Valley changed once again and became more sedentary. Throughout the region, the native people lived a rather similar lifestyle, occupying larger permanent villages near rivers and large streams in some areas and occupying broad upland ridges in other areas. Their village sites were often protected by palisades constructed of wooden posts.

During this period, people began to use crushed mussel shell to temper their pottery and continued to use the bow and arrow developed during the latter part of the Woodland period for hunting. At this time, the people were farmers growing corn, beans and squash, known as the Three Sisters, as well as sunflower and other plants. This became what archaeologists recognize as the Late Prehistoric and Protohistoric periods.

The Late Prehistoric period, as designated by archaeologists, is pre-European contact, and the Protohistoric or Contact period refers to archaeological sites occupied after European contact in the Southeast where European trade items such as European metal (copper or brass) and glass trade beads are found. In the Ohio Valley, including West Virginia, contact is thought of as beginning around 1539, when Hernando de Soto arrived in the southeastern area of North America. Soon after, European trade items began making their way inland along established trade routes between inland native groups and those living in coastal areas. At this time, European populations were living near the coast and had not yet visited inland areas like West Virginia or the Ohio Valley. Usually in West Virginia, European trade items are not found until the late 1500s to 1600s.

EARLY EXCAVATIONS IN WEST VIRGINIA

Until 1960, when the West Virginia Geological and Economic Survey hired Dr. Edward McMichael as the West Virginia state archaeologist, archaeological excavations in West Virginia were primarily conducted by amateur or avocational archaeologists, many of whom were members of the West Virginia Archeological Society (WVAS). Several of these individuals published their findings in the *West Virginia Archeologist*, the journal of the WVAS. Many times, that is the only existing information about the site. While some of these individuals recorded details and kept meticulous notes, other excavations were sometimes lacking in documentation.

National Historic Preservation Act of 1966 (NHPA) and Section 106

Section 106 of the National Historic Preservation Act requires federal agencies to evaluate the impact of all federally funded or permitted projects on historic properties, including historic buildings and archaeological sites. It also requires consultation with federally recognized Indian tribes who may have had a prehistoric presence in the area when prehistoric human remains might be impacted by the project.

Native American Graves Protection and Repatriation Act

In 1990, the Native American Graves Protection and Repatriation Act, or NAGPRA, was enacted into law by President George H.W. Bush. NAGPRA gave federally recognized Indian tribes the ability to claim human remains and associated artifacts found on federal or tribal land for reburial if the tribe could prove a direct lineal descent or cultural affiliation with the remains in question. This also applies to archaeological projects with federal funding where human remains are found.

Until recently, NAGPRA had not been implemented in West Virginia. This is primarily because there are no federally recognized Native American tribes living here, and it has not yet been possible to establish the identities of most of the native peoples who lived here before European contact or who their descendants might be. Therefore, the Native American remains that have been found in West Virginia have been considered *culturally unidentifiable* under NAGPRA. Culturally unidentifiable refers to human remains and associated funerary objects in museum or federal agency collections for which no lineal descendant or culturally affiliated Indian tribe or Native Hawaiian organization has been identified through the inventory process.

However, since the passage of NAGPRA and the National Historic Preservation Act of 1966, archaeological projects with federal funding must include consultation with federally recognized Indian tribes with a possible prehistoric presence in West Virginia to determine how to proceed when human remains might be impacted.

Until the passage of the West Virginia burial law in 1991, there were no state laws in West Virginia addressing the excavation of human remains unless the project had federal funding. WV Code §29-1-8a, Protection of Human Skeletal Remains, Grave Artifacts and Grave Markers Permits for Excavation and Removal, offers some penalties for the indiscriminate removal of human remains unless conducted by professional individuals who have applied for and received a permit from the West Virginia State Historic Preservation Office. Removal of human remains without this permit is considered a felony.

TRINOMIALS

The three-part number and letter designations that represent recorded archaeological sites are called trinomials. The trinomial designation system was developed by the Smithsonian Institution in the 1930s and 1940s. The first number represents the state in which the site is located. West Virginia is represented by the number 46. The second part represents the county. The third part is the number of the recorded site in chronological sequence. For example, 46MR001 represents the Grave Creek Mound, the first site recorded in Marshall County, West Virginia. When a site is recorded with the West Virginia State Historic Preservation Office, a unique trinomial designation is recorded.

Chapter 2

THE WOODLAND PERIOD IN THE OHIO VALLEY

In the Ohio Valley, the Woodland period is divided into Early, Middle and Late subperiods. Most mounds constructed in this region are associated with the Early Woodland Adena and Middle Woodland Hopewell cultural traditions. There was a near cessation of mound building during the Late Woodland.

EARLY WOODLAND (1000 BC TO 100 BC)

Traditionally, the beginning of Early Woodland in the Ohio Valley has been defined as the occurrence of three cultural developments: the first domesticated plants, the first clay pottery and the first burial mounds. Although archaeologists have known for some time that the use of domesticated plants dates back to the Late Archaic period, ceramic pottery manufacture and the construction of earthen burial mounds have continued to be considered hallmarks of the Early Woodland period.[4] Archaeologists working in the region have typically attached the beginning of pottery manufacture to the early part of the period at about 1000 BC and the earliest mound construction to Adena beginning in the middle part of the period at 500 to 400 BC.[5] However, current evidence indicates that at least in some areas of the Upper Ohio Valley, pottery was being produced several centuries prior to 1000 BC,[6] and at least a small number of mounds were being constructed prior to Adena, as exemplified by the Munson Springs mound in Licking County, Ohio, dated to approximately 750 BC.[7]

Much of what we know about Early Woodland societies in the region is based on work conducted at mound and non-mound mortuary sites and, to a much lesser extent, habitation sites. For this reason, Early Woodland has often been treated as being synonymous with Adena, while it is now clear that about half the period predated Adena. However, from the evidence that is available, it appears that during this period people in the Upper Ohio Valley lived in small social groups of perhaps fifteen to thirty people; occupied and used a diverse range of natural settings, including both valleys and uplands; practiced horticultural gardening as an important part of their diets; developed a complex mortuary program that utilized areas/sites geographically separated from their small "villages" or hamlets. These elements combined culminated in what archaeologists recognize as Adena.

Domesticated Plants

Long before the diets of Native Americans in the Upper Ohio Valley were reliant on corn, beans and squash beginning at around AD 1000, a different group of crops was being cultivated by small groups throughout the region. Termed the Eastern Agricultural Complex by archaeologists, these early domesticates included weedy plants with seeds high in oils, protein and/or starch. Important early domesticates included squash, sunflower, may grass, goosefoot, knotweed, sump weed, marsh elder, amaranth and Chenopodium.[8] Although Early Woodland peoples were still leading a primarily hunting-gathering or Archaic way of life based on the taking of game and the collecting of nuts and berries, they increasingly supplemented their diets with these early domesticates.

Plant domestication in the Ohio Valley may have occurred almost by accident. It probably began with the women of the group gathering fruits, nuts and edible plants for food. Some of the seeds were discarded with the village refuse. If the group returned to the same campsite the next year, they might have noticed their favorite plants growing there. At some point, they pulled unwanted weeds and planted seeds of the desired plants intentionally. Although this process no doubt took place over time, in effect, these plants were being genetically engineered and would eventually develop into new varieties.[9]

Clay Pottery

As plants were being domesticated and the native people were becoming more sedentary, clay pottery vessels for storing seeds and cooking began to appear. The earliest ceramic pottery in the Ohio Valley were large, thick-walled vessels tempered with crushed rock or grit. The type of stone used for temper depended on what was available in the area. Adding temper to the wet clay helps reduce shrinking and cracking of the clay while drying and firing. The vessels usually had wide mouths, thick walls and flat bases and sometimes heavy lug handles. The surface of the vessel was sometimes roughened with cordmarking by patting the surface of the vessel with a cord-wrapped paddle before firing. This helped prevent the container from slipping when wet. Less frequently, vessels were decorated with incised juxtaposed concentric or "nested" diamonds.[10] Prior to this, during the end of the Archaic period, native peoples in some areas of the Upper Ohio Valley, including the Kanawha Valley near Charleston, were using cooking vessels made of steatite, or soapstone, which would have been imported or traded into the area, while also manufacturing similar forms from locally available sandstone.

The first known clay pottery in eastern North America was made in the Southeast at around 2000 BC. The age of ceramic pottery in the Upper Ohio Valley is not clearly understood, although there is a growing body of evidence to support its presence during the Late Archaic in Ohio, West Virginia and areas downriver.[11]

Burial Mounds

In the Upper Ohio Valley, the first burial mounds were constructed during the Early Woodland period. Historically they were thought to have their origin with Adena at about 1000 BC; however, with new information, our current understanding is that the Adena mounds date to the latter half of the Early Woodland period, with the first examples constructed around 500 to 400 BC. We also now know that at least in some areas, small earthen mounds that predate Adena were constructed by around 750 BC.[12] Many Adena mounds were not built during a single construction episode but rather are the result of multiple episodes of use and construction dating over many decades or a few centuries.

Early Woodland people were becoming sedentary and beginning to settle into small dispersed villages or "hamlets." At least by the latter half of the period, with the rise of Adena, these "villages" were made up of a few circular post structures thought to have been interlaced with twigs and perhaps covered with bark and were not permanent. A typical structure would have been approximately ten to fifteen feet in diameter.[13] The population of a given site is believed to have been in the range of approximately fifteen to twenty individuals, with some being larger than others and possibly having populations of up to thirty people. Unfortunately, very few Adena habitation sites, or villages, have been investigated in the Upper Ohio Valley and, in particular, West Virginia.

MIDDLE WOODLAND
(CIRCA 100 BC TO AD 400)

The Middle Woodland period is typically associated with the Hopewell cultural tradition in the Upper Ohio Valley. Developing out of Adena in Ohio, the Hopewell culture flourished, with many large earthworks and mounds being constructed. Hopewell peoples also traded widely to acquire exotic materials, including copper, mica, marine shell, high-grade chert, obsidian, quartz crystal, galena and other materials including, on occasion, silver. This system of trade and interaction is known as the Hopewell Interaction Sphere.[14] Much of the exotic material acquired through long-distance trade was deposited in the graves of high-status individuals in mounds. A distinctive technologic characteristic of Hopewell was the core and blade technology, where pieces of high-quality chert, often Vanport/Flint Ridge from central Ohio, were shaped into cores from which specialized small, parallel-sided microblades were detached. Unlike their Adena predecessors, Hopewell peoples lived near their mounds and earthworks—their public spaces.

In West Virginia, the extent of Hopewell influence is uncertain, but it does not appear to have been substantial. Artifacts have been found that are considered Hopewell, but large geometric earthworks are not common. However, the group of mounds in the Kanawha Valley described by Cyrus Thomas, who directed the mound explorations in the 1880s for the Smithsonian Institution, was described as the "Ancient Works Near Charleston." Thomas spoke of "fifty mounds" and "some eight or ten enclosures containing from less than 1 to fully 30 acres."[15]

However, although there might have been some interaction between Hopewell groups in the Ohio Valley and Middle Woodland period peoples in West Virginia, there are no known mound sites that are considered by archaeologists to be Hopewell.

Chapter 3
THE ADENA CULTURE

The name *Adena* comes from an Early Woodland burial mound on the estate of Ohio governor Thomas Worthington in Chillicothe, Ohio. Governor Worthington named his estate Adena from the Hebrew word *Adina*. Excavated in 1901 by William C. Mills, curator of the Ohio State Archaeological and Historical Society, the Adena mound became the type-site of the mound-building Adena culture. The peak of Adena activity in the Upper Ohio Valley appears to have been between 200 and 100 BC. It was during this period that the largest Adena mound in the Americas, the Grave Creek Mound, in Moundsville, West Virginia, was constructed.[16]

The Adena were not a single people but instead represent a cultural tradition that may have included several related societies that participated in a shared tradition of burial ceremonialism and mound construction, with some differences noted between drainage valleys and across regions. Characteristics of the Adena cultural tradition in the Ohio Valley include burial mound construction, mortuary ceremonialism and high-status artifacts such as tubular smoking pipes; semi-keeled gorgets; quadriconcave gorgets; expanding center gorgets; Adena projectile points; hematite celts; copper bracelets and gorgets; and Adena Plain, Fayette Thick and Montgomery Incised pottery.[17]

The Adena people lived in small, loosely organized villages containing circular houses with conical roofs constructed of poles, willows and bark. Sites interpreted as Adena by archaeologists are most common in southern

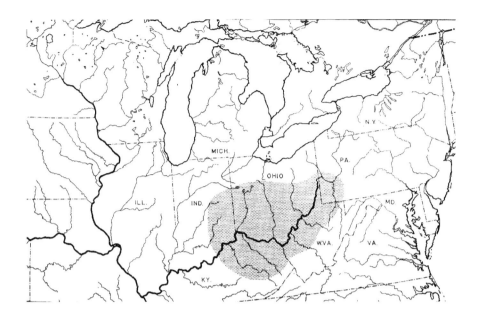

Map showing area of Adena occupation in the Ohio Valley. From Dragoo, "Mounds for the Dead." *Copyright Carnegie Institute, Carnegie Museum of Natural History.*

Ohio, eastern Indiana, the Ohio and Kanawha Valley regions of West Virginia and parts of eastern and central Kentucky, including the Bluegrass.

Sometime after 500 BC, the Adena people began burying their honored dead in conical earthen burial mounds. It is thought from the relatively small number of burials found in the mounds that only certain individuals were buried there. Because most of the population was buried elsewhere, it is likely that those interred in the mounds were individuals with some status in the community.

In addition to being burial places, Adena mounds might also have served as territorial markers, as they would have been visible on the landscape. Some Adena mounds, and in particular the larger ones, are accretional in that they were constructed in stages over time. The beginning of the mound-building sequence may have occurred when someone, possibly an important person in the community, died and was buried. Over time, other individuals died and were buried there, with additional layers of soil being added to the mound. Sometimes the original burials were cremations. Other times, the primary or first individual was buried in a log tomb or crypt.

William Webb (1940), one of the early contributors to Adena studies, first noted that the remnants of houses or buildings were beneath some

Adena mounds in the Central Ohio Valley. The structures were circular with paired posts that leaned outward. It was not until much later that these structures were determined to be mortuary or "special purpose" non-residential buildings.[18]

Adena Material Culture

Lithics

Lithics refers to tools and other objects and ornaments made from stone. The most common type of stone material used by Native Americans was chert or flint. Because it breaks like glass with naturally sharp edges, it provided an ideal material for the manufacture of piercing and cutting tools, including spear or projectile points and knives. Several types or styles of projectile points are attributed to the Adena cultural tradition, which, in order of decreasing age, have been identified as Cresap, Adena and Robbins.

Leaf-shaped or teardrop-shaped bifaces are sometimes considered "cache" blades that were buried for future use. They might have been retrieved at a later time and reworked into spear points. Some caches of blades or bifaces have also been found that might have been ceremonial "offerings" to a particular deity. These types of caches have been found in Ohio, where caches of bifaces have been found in bogs.[19]

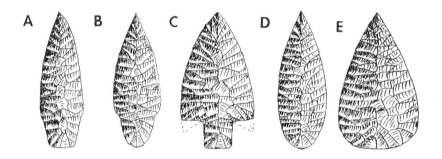

Adena projectile points: A. Cresap stemmed; B. Adena ovate-base stemmed; C. Robbins stemmed; D. Adena leaf-shaped; and E. Robbins leaf-shaped. From Dragoo, "Mounds for the Dead." *Copyright Carnegie Institute, Carnegie Museum of Natural History.*

Adena Pottery

Adena Plain pottery consists of jars with wide mouths. The height is typically about one and one-half times that of the diameter. The exterior surfaces are usually smoothed, but examples of cordmarked and punctated treatments are also known. Vessels have flat bases, and the rims are typically thicker than the body of the vessel. Thickness ranges from approximately four millimeters to fourteen millimeters, with the mean thickness being eight to nine millimeters. Other Early Woodland types sharing technological and/or stylistic similarities with Adena pottery include McKees Rock Plain and Montgomery Incised.[20]

Smoking Pipes

Another item commonly found in Adena mounds is the smoking pipe. Pipes were typically made from stone or clay. Throughout prehistory and among historic American Indian peoples, smoking was both a religious and personal event. The earliest pipes found in West Virginia were in Adena mounds and may have had a ceremonial function or may have belonged to the individuals interred in the mound. Smoking pipes were found with many burials, predominantly those of males. In addition to ceremonial uses, these pipes appear to have been personal items that were used by men throughout life and accompanied them in death.

In the Ohio Valley, smoking pipes have been associated with Early Woodland cultures from 1000 BC to AD 200.[21] The earliest pipes were tubular ground stone pipes.[22] The shape and style of smoking pipes changed from tubular pipes during the Early Woodland period to platform pipes during the Middle Woodland period.[23] Platform pipes are typically associated with the Ohio Valley Hopewell, where most were found. Sometimes the bowl of the pipe was replaced by an animal form. Platform pipes are found throughout the Eastern Woodlands and were among the items traded through the Hopewell Interaction Sphere. During the Late Woodland period and later, elbow pipes began to appear.[24]

Copper Artifacts

A variety of copper objects and ornaments have been found in Adena mounds throughout the Ohio Valley. Rolled copper beads, copper strips, gorgets, breastplates and rolled copper bracelets and rings have been found. Thought to originate in the Great Lakes region, native copper was made into ornaments as early as the Late Archaic period.

Gorgets and Pendants

Ornaments such as gorgets (with two holes) and pendants (with one hole) that were worn around the neck have been found frequently at Adena sites. Many were made of stone, particularly out of banded slate, and copper.

Marine Shell

Both the small Marginella shell (*Prunum apicineum*) and the larger *Olivella biplicata* marine shells have been found in Adena mounds throughout the Ohio Valley, usually as beads. Both of these species of marine shells were imported from the Atlantic coast and the Gulf of Mexico. Exotic items such as marine shell indicate the long-distance trade networks between the Greater Ohio Valley and the Gulf and Atlantic coasts of North America that were in place by the Late Archaic period. Because of their exotic nature, they were no doubt considered status objects and were probably an indication of the individual's status in the community.

Tablets

Engraved stone and clay tablets of many shapes and sizes have been found in Adena mounds. Many are engraved in geometric designs. Thirteen have been found in Ohio, Kentucky and West Virginia. Only one—the Wright tablet from Montgomery County, Ohio—was found by a trained archaeologist. Typically, the engraved tablets are rectangular pieces of stone or clay with engravings on one side to create an area of relief. Two engraved tablets were found at the Lakin Mound in Mason County by an amateur archaeologist.[25]

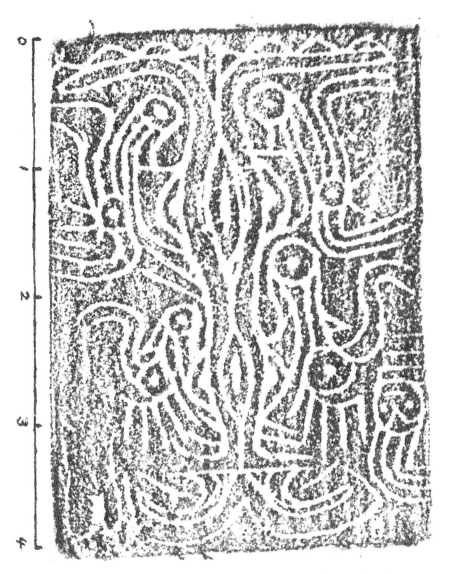

Rubbing from the Lakin Tablet from the Lakin Mound in Mason County, West Virginia. *West Virginia Archeological Society, Norona 1950.*

Birdstones

Birdstones are small abstract stone carvings made by early Native Americans usually in the form of an animal or bird. Their meaning and purpose are unknown, although they are commonly found with burials. Birdstones were found in many Early Woodland Adena mounds.

GLOSSARY

A glossary of archaeological terms is provided in the back of the book.

Chapter 4

HISTORY OF MOUND
EXPLORATIONS

In the late 1600s and 1700s, when the first Europeans crossed the Appalachian Mountains and arrived in the Ohio Valley, they soon became aware of and intrigued by the many conical earthen mounds they encountered there. Because the mounds had been constructed many hundreds of years before European contact, the native people they encountered at the time had no memory of the mound builders. The identities of the mysterious "mound builders" eluded the newcomers for many years. They thought the builders must have been some mysterious "lost race" of people and not the ancestors of the Native Americans they encountered there.[26]

It was not until 1881 that a Division of Mound Exploration of the Smithsonian Institution's Bureau of Ethnology was formed to investigate the identities of the mysterious mound builders. Cyrus Thomas was eventually appointed to lead the research program of the Division of Mound Explorations. The primary goal was to resolve the debate over the identity of the "mound builders." According to Thomas, "The most important question to be settled is, 'were the mounds built by the Indians?' The Director of the Bureau of Ethnology was desirous, therefore, that this important question, the origin of the mounds, should if possible be definitely settled, as it is the pivot on which all the other problems must turn."[27]

Thomas also noted four secondary objectives:

1. To identify the variation in form or shape of the structures and "develop a comprehensive mound classification system";
2. To investigate and describe the mode of construction of the different mound types;
3. To establish a system of regional archaeological districts that reflected the geographical range of the various mound types; and
4. To obtain a representative artifact assemblage.

Another goal of the mound explorations was to establish a "detailed and objective data base that would be available and of value to future generations of archaeologists."[28]

In developing a plan for the mound explorations, the main problem for Thomas was that the prehistoric mounds were located throughout the eastern United States. A budget of $5,000 had been allocated to examine the mounds, and it wasn't financially feasible to examine all or even most of the many mounds. Instead, Thomas chose a research design that involved the selection and detailed examination of a sample of mounds "that represented the full range of known variation of form and mode of construction, and which were distributed over wide geographical area." The research design formulated by Thomas included a "sampling strategy" to "obtain systematic geographic coverage of mounds throughout the eastern United States."[29]

Thomas used published accounts of mounds and correspondence collected by the Smithsonian Institution concerning mounds over the years to select mounds to be examined. He also selected a sample of mounds from his earlier publication, *Bulletin 12 of the Bureau of Ethnology, Catalogue of Prehistoric Works East of the Rocky Mountains*.[30]

Thomas was rarely in the field himself but instead chose three field assistants to perform the excavations. In West Virginia, his field assistant was Colonel P.W. Norris, who also visited Arkansas, the Dakotas, Kentucky, Iowa, Minnesota, Missouri, Ohio and Texas.[31]

The resulting *Report on the Mound Explorations of the Bureau of Ethnology* by Thomas concluded that the ancestors of living Native Americans in the United States had constructed the mounds. The mound explorations were also considered the beginning of modern archaeology in America.[32]

Chapter 5

MOUND SITES IN WEST VIRGINIA

BEECH BOTTOM MOUND (46BR003)

The Beech Bottom Mound in Brooke County, West Virginia, was located fourteen miles north of Wheeling, West Virginia, on the Ohio River at Beech Bottom on property owned by the Wheeling Steel Corporation. The site was brought to the attention of the Museum of the University of Pennsylvania by an employee of the company.[33]

The mound was partially excavated in 1930 by Charles Bache and Linton Satterthwaite Jr. At the time of excavation, the mound was thirteen feet high and seventy feet in diameter. The excavators thought "the mound was built as a unit—if not at one time, at least according to one plan."[34]

At the time of excavation, the mound was conical, although one side had been dug into. Excavations began on July 3, 1930. An arbitrary datum point was selected outside the mound, and a 1.0-meter trench was dug from the datum point into the side of the mound and then at 0.75-meter increments until it reached the top of the mound.[35]

From the top of the mound, the trench was widened, and the excavators began digging with shovels. The first object encountered was a gray pipestone tube in pieces and some red ocher. A bit lower, two stemmed bifaces, an unbroken pipestone tube and a gray banded slate gorget were found. It appeared to Bache and Satterthwaite that they were in a "rich area."[36]

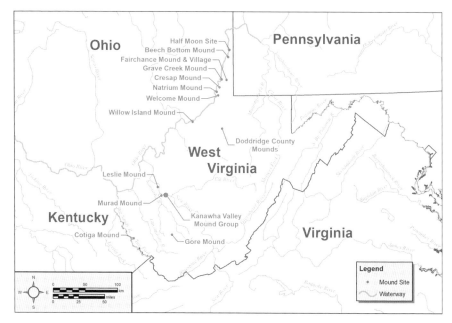

Map of West Virginia showing locations of mound sites discussed in the text. *Courtesy of Cultural Resource Analysts, Inc. and Jim Kompanek.*

Beech Bottom Mound before excavations. *Courtesy of the Penn Museum, Image 28808.*

The excavators decided to learn as much as possible about the construction of the mound before excavating the center. The cut was extended to a "pie-shaped sector," called the Main Excavation Sector, and continued in thin levels. Throughout the excavation of the sector, objects were recovered, and their positions were recorded. Objects appeared to be concentrated near the center of the mound. Because of this, the entire top of the mound was removed to a depth of half a meter. Nothing was found except pits dug by pot-hunters.[37]

Excavation continued downward on the Main Excavation Sector, and when they reached a level called 0.30, the excavators encountered a layer of yellow sand that was described as oval shaped and convex. The central area was excavated to that level. Digging proceeded using knives, trowels and brushes. They had encountered the only burial in the mound. Using small tools, they cleared the yellow sand walls and the dark earth fill surrounding the burial. From the top to the bottom of the grave, objects were encountered. There were many broken tubes and fragments, as well as broken blades.[38] According to Bache and Satterthwaite, there was "little doubt that the mound and its contents, so far as we excavated, pertains to the burial which we found."[39]

Photograph of Beech Bottom Mound after the top of the mound was removed. *Courtesy of the Penn Museum, Image 299899.*

The individual was covered with marine shell and copper beads. He was completely crushed and in poor condition. The cranium was completely disintegrated, but the jaws and bones of the face were fairly intact. All the hand and foot bones were gone except one fragment. Although Bache and Satterthwaite thought that no other subfloor features existed, they were uncertain if there were additional burials.[40]

According to Bache and Satterthwaite, the construction of the mound at Beech Bottom took place as follows. An irregular ring of dark earth was spread around what would be the base of the mound. Next, an oval pit 3.5 meters long by 1.3 meters wide and 1.4 meters deep was dug through the dark layer of soil, and the subsoil was spread over the dark soil around the pit.[41]

A lining of bark was placed in the burial pit, and an extended male individual was placed on the prepared grave on his back with his arms at his sides and legs slightly bowed. His head was turned toward the south. Several strands of discoidal shell beads and tubular beads were placed across the individual's face and neck. Upon his right shoulder was a bone flaking tool, and under his right scapula was a rough stemmed blade. Several strands of rolled copper beads and tubular shell beads were across his chest and down his left side to the hip. Copper beads and discoidal shell beads were along his right side, and copper beads were across his waist and arms above the wrist.[42]

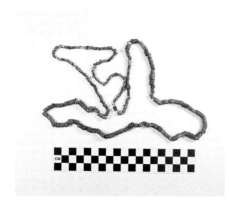

Left: Shell disk beads from the Beech Bottom Mound. *Courtesy of the Penn Museum, Object 36-16-181.*

Right: Rolled copper beads from the Beech Bottom Mound. *Courtesy of the Grave Creek Mound Archaeological Complex, West Virginia Department of Arts, Culture and History.*

Left: Animal bone and Marginella shell beads from the Beech Bottom Mound. *Courtesy of the Penn Museum, Object 36-16-178.*

Below: Marginella marine shell beads from the Beech Bottom Mound. *Courtesy of the Grave Creek Mound Archaeological Complex, West Virginia Department of Arts, Culture and History.*

Between the individual's legs and above the knees were strands of tubular and discoidal shell beads, under which was a large blocked end tubular pipe and the tip of a broken stemmed blade. The lower half of his legs and feet were covered with copper beads and a mass of copper and shell beads. Under this were a large number of Marginella and Olivella marine shell beads, as well as two beaver incisors, an eagle claw, two small rodent jaws and a broken bone "knife" thought to be the contents of a pouch or medicine bag. More beads were next to the individual's legs.[43]

Several objects were placed around the individual. A cluster of ten leaf-shaped blades and several broken pieces of blocked-end pipes were placed above his right shoulder. Above his left shoulder were four rounded-base stemmed blades and a broken blade. To the west of these objects were a blocked-end tubular pipe, a leaf-shaped blade and a piece of worked stone.[44]

Near the individual's right leg was a rounded-base stemmed blade, and across his right elbow was a tubular pipe. Near his ankles were two celts and two broken tubular pipes. Also near the individual were a bone handle, a bone flaking tool and fragments of tubular pipes. Graphite, yellow ocher and red ocher was visible on some of the items found.[45]

Because of the height and size of the buried individual, he was assumed to be an adult male. The length of the femur was approximately fifty centimeters.[46]

After the individual was buried, he was covered with a layer of yellow sand and then dark soil. Found in the soil were one hematite celt, four leaf-shaped blades, five stemmed blades, two notched points, four broken blade tips, seventeen broken sections and many small fragments of tubular pipes and four small animal bones. Also found were pieces of charcoal and dark earth.[47]

Near the top of the burial pit was another cache of objects including two complete and three broken leaf-shaped blades and a long section of a broken tubular pipe. Twenty-four small tube pieces were found nearby. Other tube sections, a leaf-shaped blade, a celt, a piece of bone and mussel shells were scattered near the cache.[48]

A dark layer of earth had been spread over the grave and the items. It appeared to be the beginning of a small primary mound. Additional items and more dark earth were added until the mound was approximately 2.6 meters above the ground. Red ocher was added to cover the burial objects and scattered through the mound. On top of the small primary mound was found a tubular pipe, fourteen blades and two lumps of red ocher. The whole dark primary mound was then covered with a thick layer of yellow soil thought to complete the mound.[49]

Tubular pipes from the Beech Bottom Mound. *Courtesy of the Penn Museum, Image 13294.*

Photograph of Beech Bottom Mound during excavations. *Courtesy of the Penn Museum, Image 299900.*

Photograph of Beech Bottom Mound during excavations. *Courtesy of the Penn Museum, Image 299901.*

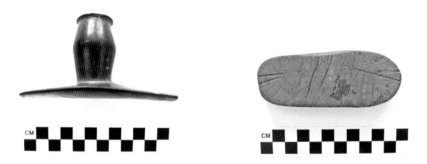

Left: Platform pipe from the Beech Bottom Mound. *Courtesy of the Penn Museum, Object 30-60-1.*

Right: Abrading stone from the Beech Bottom Mound. *Courtesy of the Penn Museum, Object 36-16-140.*

Adena bifaces from the Beech Bottom Mound. *Courtesy of the Penn Museum, Image 13293.*

Adena leaf-shaped and stemmed bifaces from the Beech Bottom Mound. *Courtesy of the Penn Museum, Image 13291.*

Top: Sphere and cups from the Beech Bottom Mound. *Courtesy of the Penn Museum, Objects 36-16-134, 36-16-135 and 36-16-136.*

Middle: Stone pendant from the Beech Bottom Mound. *Courtesy of the Penn Museum, Object 30-60-21.*

Bottom: Birdstone from the Beech Bottom Mound. *Courtesy of the Penn Museum, Object 30-60-2.*

CAMDEN PARK MOUND (46WA012)

The Camden Park Mound is located in the historic Camden Park amusement park near Huntington, West Virginia, in Wayne County. The park was created in 1903, when the Camden Interstate Railway opened between Huntington, West Virginia, and Ashland, Kentucky. A pavilion was created for picnicking, reunions and square dancing near the exchange point where Twelvepole Creek entered the Ohio River.[50]

The park was named after Senator J.N. Camden, who was also one of the railway owners. A carousel or merry-go-round and other amusement rides were added, and the park expanded for the next twenty years.[51]

The Camden Park Mound is on the floodplain near the center of the amusement park. The mound is conical and fifteen feet high and one hundred feet in diameter. It has never been excavated. Early on, a bandstand was located on top of the mound, and visitors would be entertained by music from there. After the bandstand was removed, a fence was built around the mound. The mound still has a flat top that suggests it might have been leveled at one time to accommodate the bandstand.[52]

COTIGA MOUND (46MO001)

The Cotiga Mound site was located in Mingo County, West Virginia, on the second terrace of the southeast bank of the Tug Fork River at the confluence with Miller Creek. It is also the location of the intersection of U.S. Routes 52 and 119. The mound site was purchased from the Cotiga Development Company by the West Virginia Division of Highways, giving the mound its name.[53] The Cotiga Mound was the first archaeological site recorded in Mingo County.

In the late 1970s, Jeffrey Graybill of the West Virginia Geological and Economic Survey conducted an exploratory excavation of the mound at the request of the West Virginia Department of Transportation in anticipation of the construction of U.S. 119. Before that time, not much was known about the mound.[54]

At the time of the excavations, the mound was eleven feet high and ninety feet in diameter. Several trees thought to be over one hundred years old were on the mound slopes. The mound was estimated to be approximately two thousand years old. The excavation confirmed that the mound was man-made.[55] The mound was also identified as an Adena mound.[56]

Although the Cotiga Mound was listed in the National Register of Historic Places, its location on the centerline for the proposed Corridor G (U.S. 119) meant that avoidance of the site was not feasible. Because it could not be avoided, the National Advisory Council determined that adverse effects to the mound could only be avoided by data recovery excavation, or total excavation of the mound.[57]

Excavations between 1991 and 1992 by GAI Consultants and radiocarbon dating indicated that the mound had been built in several episodes between 205 BC and AD 75. Much of its construction and use occurred in 102 BC.[58]

Fieldwork on the mound began in January 1991 and was completed in May 1992. Analyses were completed in June 1993. From the excavations and analyses, the archaeologists were able to re-create the sequence of mound-building events. The mound construction was thought to begin around 205 BC, when a layer of silty yellow soil was spread over the area to create a prepared surface for future construction.[59]

The Prepared Surface also contained artifacts from the area that included fifty-five pieces of pottery identified as Armstrong Plain that dated from 300 BC to AD 100, ten lithic tools and flakes of mica. Also recovered from the Prepared Surface soil were sweetgum, pine, seeds and walnut shells. Around the same time, several cremations were thought to have taken place in an area called the Southwest Cremation Area. Seven cremation surfaces were found there.[60]

The next phase of mortuary activity was the construction of a large, centrally located log-framed feature and a cremation within it. This was known as the Central Feature, and it was constructed on the Prepared Surface around 190 BC.[61]

At some point, a primary mound called the Central Feature Cap was constructed over the Central Feature in the center of the Prepared Surface. Next, a berm of earth was erected around the Central Feature Cap. The earthen berm supported a rock ring containing over 1,600 sandstone rocks and covered the Prepared Surface.[62]

Ramp extensions were added next that incorporated the earthen berm and the rock ring into the mound. The ramp extensions covered the inner edge of the rock ring and berm at the northern edge of the Central Feature Cap. The ramp extensions were deposited on all other areas of the submound buried A horizon.[63]

The capping continued using basket loads of earth to construct the First General Mound Cap that covered the entire area and extended into the terrace surface. Some of the basket loads of soil used for the Cap contained cremated bone from cremation surfaces elsewhere. The First General Mound Cap was dated to approximately 20 BC. Additional capping episodes were conducted over time and completed by approximately AD 75.[64]

Artifacts from the Middle Woodland and Late Prehistoric periods, a pipe and two celts, were found near the surface of the mound near the top. A date from the pipe contents was approximately AD 1290. In addition, ornaments found included two celts made from greenstone, two gorget fragments and a drilled and incised small rock. One of the gorgets was a reddish-brown slate with a polished exterior. The second gorget fragment was a dark gray slate with a black and orange-brown polished exterior. One pipe fragment and a broken, although nearly complete, smoking pipe were also found.[65]

More than twenty-five pieces of mica were found in the Cotiga Mound, many of which were microscopic. Two large sheets of mica were from Burial 13 in the Central Feature. Mica is frequently found in Adena mounds and usually in direct association with burials.[66]

Information from various analyses and radiocarbon dates suggest that most of the primary ritual activity at the mound occurred between 205 BC and 20 BC. The cultural features occurred in the lower parts of the mound.[67]

The Cotiga Mound contained the remains of between seven and eighteen cremated individuals and associated grave items. There appeared to be a range of individuals, including males, one female, infants and children. Items found with the individuals included modified animal bone, stone tools, mica and three copper bracelets.[68]

At least two paired-post structures were located under the mound with evidence that they had been built near the time of the mound construction. The structures were thought to have been used for mortuary-related activities.[69]

Copper bracelets from Cotiga Mound. *Courtesy of the Grave Creek Mound Archaeological Complex, West Virginia Department of Arts, Culture and History.*

One of the more unusual aspects of the Cotiga Mound excavations was the treatment of the human remains that were found. The West Virginia Department of Transportation had entered into an agreement with the West Virginia Committee on Native North American Archaeological and Burial Policies that all of the remains and associated burial items would be reburied. Although a lawsuit was filed by the Council for West Virginia Archaeology and other interested parties to prevent reburial, the remains were reburied. This was the first time in West Virginia that Native American remains from a state project with federal funding were reburied.[70]

CRESAP MOUND (46MR007)

The Cresap Mound was located on Cresap Bottom in Marshall County approximately six and a half miles downriver from Moundsville, West Virginia. The property was owned by the Cresap family until it was sold to Hanna Coal Company. For many years, the family had protected the mound from disturbance and looting. Artifacts from many periods were found on much of Cresap Bottom. Two additional smaller mounds were located several thousand feet south of the Cresap Mound. Both appeared to have been previously excavated.[71]

At some point, the mound and surrounding land were transferred to the West Virginia Highway Department to create a park along WV Route 2, with the condition that the mound would be protected. In 1958, the highway department relocated Route 2, and the park with the mound was transferred to Hanna Coal Company, which had plans to build an industrial plant in the area.[72]

When Delf Norona of the WVAS learned of the proposed construction that might impact the mound, he enlisted the aid of Sigfus Olafson, president of the WVAS, and Reverend Clifford Lewis, secretary of the WVAS, to ensure the mound would be excavated scientifically.[73]

The WVAS members contacted Hanna Coal Company, the West Virginia Department of Highways and the Carnegie Museum in Pittsburgh to develop a plan for excavation of the mound. Don Dragoo, curator with the Carnegie Museum, would direct the excavations. With cooperation between these parties, a plan of action was created, and excavations began on June 2, 1958.[74]

Hanna Coal Company was very supportive of the project and offered four men to help with the excavations. The company also provided plastic sheets to protect the excavations from rain. The West Virginia Highway Department arranged for fencing to protect the mound while it was being excavated.[75] In addition, William Reeves from the Carnegie Museum staff assisted with the photography during the excavations.[76]

All of the vegetation was removed from the surface of the mound and surrounding area. Shrubs around the base of the mound were more than ten feet high at the time of excavation. A locust tree on top of the mound was removed, but the roots had grown through the mound to the bottom and had disturbed most of the burials inside except for those below the floor of the mound.[77]

At the time of excavation, the Cresap Mound was fifteen feet high and approximately seventy feet in diameter. The only evidence of previous disturbance was from tree roots and groundhog burrows. A grid of ten-by-ten-foot squares was established over the mound and surrounding area.[78] Next, a ten-by-fifty-foot trench was dug along the north–south axis approximately thirty to forty feet west of the center of the mound, exposing the level of the topsoil and underlying subsoil surrounding the mound. Digging began at the outer portion of the southwest quarter of the mound. Hoes were used for digging, following the contours of the mound in one-inch layers. Once a feature or burial was encountered, smaller tools and trowels were used.[79]

At a depth of 1.5 feet below the top of the mound, the excavators encountered an old humus layer 0.3 to 0.5 feet thick. The zone was interpreted as the surface of a large inner mound. The southwest quarter of the inner mound was excavated, and the first features and burials were found on the surface of this inner mound.[80]

It appeared to Dragoo that the layer of soil directly above the Inner Mound had been added to cover the burials but had been added after a "lapse of considerable time after the completion of the inner mound." The Inner Mound had been built over a structure described as a "charnel house" with a central fire pit containing ashes and burned stones. A prepared circular clay floor surrounded the pit. Around the clay floor was a ditch that contained charcoal, burned earth, bone and shell.[81]

According to Dragoo, the first burial in the mound was an individual buried within the structure in a shallow subfloor pit just west of the central fire pit. A "crematory basin" and two extended adult burials were also added, and these were covered with a layer of dark earth. Gradually, additional

Photograph of "Inner Mound" after the top zone had been removed from the southeast portion of the Cresap Mound. From Dragoo, "Mounds for the Dead." *Copyright Carnegie Institute, Carnegie Museum of Natural History.*

burials were added and covered with more earth until the small mound was 4.75 feet in height. Dragoo called this the West Primary Mound.[82]

Later, a second area south of the fire pit was used, and a crematory basin containing six individuals and two individual burials was added. These were also covered with earth, forming a small mound approximately 3.1 feet high.[83] Dragoo called this the Second Primary Mound.

Next, an area east of the central fire pit was selected and another burial was placed in the clay floor of the structure. Another small mound was formed over this approximately 5.3 feet high that contained eight additional burials. This mound was called the South Primary Mound. Charcoal particles were found on the surfaces and around the edges of these small mounds that led Dragoo to think that the surrounding structure might have been burned at this time.[84]

After the three primary mounds were created and reached a certain height, additional burials, features and added soil created the "main mound" that was approximately fifteen feet high.[85] Thirty-one features and fifty-four burials were encountered during excavations of the Cresap Mound. Some of the features also contained burials. Features included crematory basins, subfloor tombs, clay floor, fire pits and prepared areas for burials.[86]

Of the fifty-four individuals found in the Cresap Mound, forty-five were adults, four were children and five were cremations that appeared to be adult. Among the burials, there were sixteen men, three women and thirty-five unidentifiable individuals. However, in addition to the fifty-four burials encountered, fragmentary unburned bone and pieces of calcined bone found throughout the mound suggest that there might have been more burials. Of the fifty-four individuals in the mound, burial items were found in association with thirty-four of them. Red ocher was found with thirty-one burials.[87]

A total of 796 artifacts was found in the Cresap Mound. Of these, 133 were polished stone, 141 were chipped stone, 373 were copper, 23 were bone, 115 were shell, 9 were pottery sherds and 2 were miscellaneous.[88]

Assorted bifaces from the Cresap Mound. A. Cresap bifaces from features in the mound floor; B. Robbins bifaces from the top zone of the mound; C. Flat-base, straight-stemmed bifaces from the lower and middle zones of the mound; D. Adena leaf-shaped bifaces from the lower and middle zones of the mound; E. Adena bifaces from the lower and middle zones of the mound. From Dragoo, "Mounds for the Dead." *Copyright Carnegie Institute, Carnegie Museum of Natural History.*

Drills and scrapers from the Cresap Mound. From Dragoo, "Mounds for the Dead." *Copyright Carnegie Institute, Carnegie Museum of Natural History.*

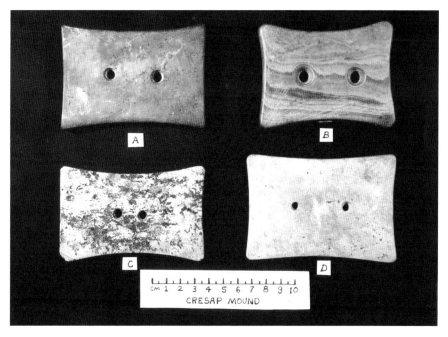

Gorgets from the Cresap Mound. From Dragoo, "Mounds for the Dead." *Copyright Carnegie Institute, Carnegie Museum of Natural History.*

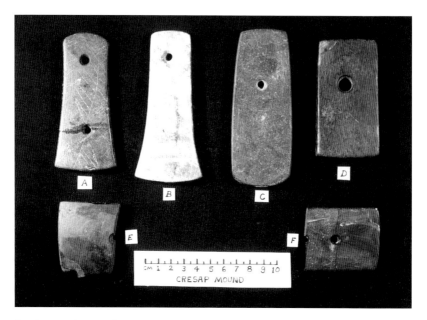

Pendants and gorget from the Cresap Mound. From Dragoo, "Mounds for the Dead." *Copyright Carnegie Institute, Carnegie Museum of Natural History.*

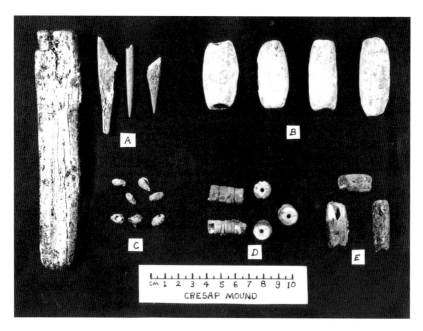

Bone and shell artifacts from the Cresap Mound. A. Bone spatula and awls; B. Large marine shell beads; C. Marginella shell beads; D. Disk shell beads; E. Small marine shell beads. From Dragoo, "Mounds for the Dead." *Copyright Carnegie Institute, Carnegie Museum of Natural History.*

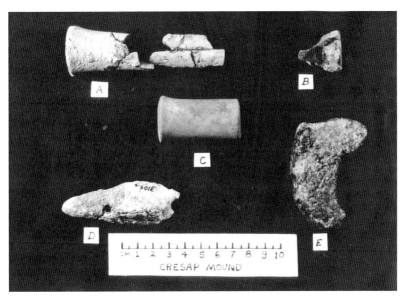

Pipes and boatstones from the Cresap Mound. From Dragoo, "Mounds for the Dead." *Copyright Carnegie Institute. Carnegie Museum of Natural History.*

Hemispheres and stone spheres from various features in the Cresap Mound. From Dragoo, "Mounds for the Dead." *Copyright Carnegie Institute, Carnegie Museum of Natural History.*

Reconstructed turtle effigy tablet from Cresap Mound. *Courtesy of the Carnegie Museum of Natural History.*

DODDRIDGE COUNTY MOUNDS (46DO001–46DO005)

Five burial mounds were found in Doddridge County, West Virginia, near Buckeye Creek and Meat House Fork, tributaries of Middle Island Creek. Two mounds, designated DO-1 and DO-2, were on a steep hill overlooking the town of Morgansville and about five miles east of the county seat of Doddridge County, West Union.[89]

The three other mounds, designated DO-3, DO-4 and DO-5, were on a terrace north of Meathouse Fork. West Virginia Route 18 is parallel to the stream. Mound DO-3 is near the village of Blandville and was slightly damaged during road construction. Mound DO-4 is located approximately half a mile down Meathouse Fork on a high bluff overlooking a bend in the stream and about three miles south of West Union near the junction of West Union and Smithburg Roads. Mound DO-5 is located on a bluff at the junction of Eibscamp Run and Meathouse Fork above Blandville.[90]

In 1929, Ernest Sutton conducted excavations of Mound DO-2. At the time, the mound was approximately ten feet high and seventy-five feet in diameter and was the largest mound in the group. Sutton referred to Mound DO-2 as the Zahn-Maxwell Mound, as approximately two-thirds of the structure was on the farm belonging to Ben Zahn and Lewis Maxwell and one-third was on the Maxwell farm.[91]

A large black walnut tree, approximately eighteen inches in diameter, was in the center of the mound. Other bushes were around the tree. The mound was also covered with a layer of rocks. Once the rocks were removed, a two-foot excavation was begun. Digging deeper, a subsoil of hard clay was encountered. The soil above the hard layer was streaked with dark organic material and bits of ash and charcoal. The excavation was widened, and using a mattock and shovel, the excavators dug deeper. At approximately five feet deep, the mattock broke two black chert bifaces.[92]

Approximately one foot deeper, four pieces of human bone were encountered. Red and yellow ocher was present. The position of the bone, which was thought to be parts of ribs and arm bones, and the ocher suggested that an extended burial had been placed there.[93]

Two additional openings were made toward the north side of the mound. Each opening encountered skeletal material that suggested extended burials. In addition, a hematite hemisphere, a gorget, and a 3-inch circular disc, a dark chert biface, and two rectangular sandstone "polishing stones" were found.[94]

In a fourth opening on the north side of the mound, a well-preserved individual surrounded by puddled clay was encountered. It appeared that the individual had been enclosed in the puddled clay, which had then been baked or heated.[95]

Mound DO-1, also known as the Zahn Mound, was also opened. This mound was approximately one hundred feet west of DO-2 and was approximately twelve feet in diameter at the base and three feet high. It appeared that the mound had been impacted by cultivation, and there was some question about whether it was man-made. However, excavation revealed an individual placed in a sitting position on a large flat rock with the legs extended toward the larger mound. Beneath the large rock was a brown, powdery material thought to have been the remains of clothing. Below the material were found four blades, three of which were broken; two pieces of a pipe; a chert scraper; a bluish-gray banner stone in two pieces; a small black biface; and a bone needle or awl about five inches long that was broken into four pieces. No further work was conducted at the site after the property owner, Mr. Zahn, asked them to discontinue.[96]

Mound DO-3, also known as the Bland Mound near Blandville, was conical in shape and approximately twenty-five feet in diameter and three feet high. An entry was made on the north side of the mound, and ashes, burned bone, charcoal, two hematite celts, one black and white granite celt and a bluish-white chert biface were found. A later excavation at the mound on the south side revealed paired postholes and loaded dirt.[97]

Mound DO-4, also known as the Gabbert Mound, was a rather large mound that had been almost completely destroyed by pot hunters looking for artifacts. Originally, it was thought to be sixty feet in diameter and ten to twelve feet high. Excavation of the mound recovered bone fragments thought to be from cremation burials.[98]

FAIRCHANCE MOUND AND VILLAGE (46MR013)

The Fairchance Mound and village sites near Moundsville, West Virginia, were thought to be occupied during the early Middle Woodland period, around AD 100 to 200. The village site covered approximately one acre next to a burial mound on Middle Grave Creek approximately two miles from the Ohio River.[99]

Between 1962 and 1964, the Fairchance Mound was excavated by members of the Wheeling Chapter of the WVAS. In 1975, the Fairchance village was investigated by the West Virginia Geological and Economic Survey. The Fairchance site provided a large amount of information about early Middle Woodland occupation and mortuary ceremonialism for the Upper Ohio Valley. It appears that the site was intensively occupied during the second century AD. Preservation at the site was very good.[100]

The Fairchance village was located in a small area of about one acre. The mound was located approximately one hundred feet to the southwest of the village. Both were situated approximately three hundred feet from Middle Grave Creek, and the site location suggested it was probably subjected to periodic flooding.[101]

In 1962, when the excavations of the mound were underway, it was visited by archaeologist Dr. Edward McMichael. Originally, the mound was seven to eight feet high, according to local residents, but it had been reduced by plowing to a low circular elevation.[102]

The Fairchance Mound was oval and measured 65.0 feet southwest by northeast and 50.0 feet northwest by southeast. The deepest mound fill was 2.2 feet and consisted of local silty clay loam, village debris and stone slabs.[103]

The floor of the mound contained a layer of sand up to two inches thick covering village features and debris. The mound contained a stone subfloor rectangular tomb for what was thought to be the principal internment (Burial 17) southwest of the center of the mound and two oval stone vaults for Burials 14 and 28. There were several other stone slabs at various locations throughout the mound.[104]

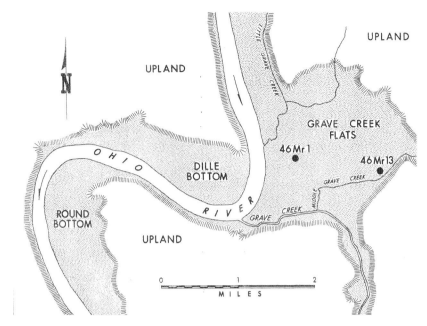

Map showing locations of Fairchance Mound and Village (46MR013) in relation to the Grave Creek Mound (46MR001). *West Virginia Archeological Society, Hemmings, "Fairchance Mound."*

Burial 17 had "fine cut marks across the frontal and parietal/temporal bones on both sides of the skull," suggesting to McMichael that it could be "one of the earliest instances of scalping in the Eastern United States."[105]

There were forty-nine burials in the Fairchance Mound. The mound contained adults of both sexes, juveniles and infants. Some were buried in log tombs, some in stone-lined tombs and some in bark-covered graves or in mound fill.[106]

The Fairchance village is one of the only known habitation sites associated with a burial mound in West Virginia. The 1975 excavation by the WVAS of the Fairchance village area uncovered thirty features, scattered postmolds and one burial, that of a fetus.[107] The village was abundant with artifacts, floral and faunal remains and debris, much like the mound fill. Features and postmolds were densely concentrated and even overlapping in some areas. The excavators were unable to trace the postmold patterns of houses or other structures; however, it appeared from the size of the posts and impressions of wall material on mud dauber nests that the houses were substantial. Features included hearths, storage pits and refuse pits. A bell-shaped storage pit of about five cubic feet was used and reused for refuse.[108]

Plant remains from the Fairchance village included charred/carbonized seeds and nutshell, wood charcoal and bark. The results of the floral analysis identified the following types of plant remains: nuts: acorns, black walnut, shagbark hickory, butternut, pignut, oak and shellbark hickory; fruits: wild plum, sumac, ground cherry and honey locust; and grain seeds: amaranth, marsh elder (?) and legume seeds.[109]

Pottery found at the village included the remains of one or two Watson cordmarked utility vessels.[110]

Faunal remains from the village included mammals, predominantly white-tailed deer, as well as elk, racoon, squirrel, woodchuck, gray fox, beaver, black bear, river otter, muskrat, rabbit, chipmunk and prairie mole. Birds represented were turkey, Canada goose and passenger pigeon. Reptiles found were turtles, including box turtle, soft-shelled turtle and snapping turtle.[111]

No dog remains were recovered from the village, but a few were recovered from the mound.[112] Nine species of mussels were found. All species would have been found in large streams with swift currents and gravel bottoms. In this area, it would have been the Ohio River or large local streams.[113] Amphibians found were Hellbender and frog or toad. Fish included drumfish and Redhorse sucker.[114]

In 1963, a radiocarbon date was received of 1790± 150 BP or AD 173. The sample was taken from decayed wood from what was thought to be a central tomb and one of the earliest burials in the mound (Burial 17, Feature 9). With the "sitting" individual were found various celts, pendants, gorgets and shell beads. All the artifacts were considered typical Middle Woodland.[115]

The individuals recovered from the Fairchance Mound included forty-four persons. Although forty-nine burials were excavated, some of the remains were not preserved or collected. Analyses of the individuals from the mound allowed several conclusions to be made about the health of the population at the Fairchance site. The burial population consisted of twenty-two males, ten females and twelve juveniles of indeterminate sex.[116] Infant mortality was relatively low at 11 percent, and life expectancy was good for the time. For men, life expectancy was forty-five to fifty-five, which was considered old for the time.[117]

No signs of violence were noted, and death would probably have been from natural causes. One male individual was thought to be over eighty years of age and in good physical condition, although life expectancy to that age would have been extremely rare.[118]

Gore Mound (46BO026)

The Gore Mound is located on a slightly elevated area of narrow stream terrace of Hewitt Creek in Boone County, West Virginia. Before excavations, what appeared to be a low earthen mound measured approximately two and a half feet high by thirty feet in diameter. The mound was covered by a layer of earth that concealed the rock fill that was previously exposed. An earlier property owner had covered the rock with earth.[119]

In 1975, WVAS members Sigfus Olafson and Don Jarvis were notified of the impending destruction of the mound by property owner Darrel Gore, who planned to level out the property. With the cooperation of Mr. Gore, excavations were conducted by WVAS members and volunteer labor from members of the local community.[120]

A five-foot-wide test trench was excavated through the center of the mound in a north–south direction. At the center of the mound was a large sassafras tree stump that prevented excavations there. Nothing of significance was found in the trench, and the excavation was expanded. Eventually, 80 percent of the mound was removed by hand, with the rock covering removed with power equipment.[121]

Initially, a central pit had been dug into the ground and the floor and sides lined with slabs of stone. A mound of stone and earth was then erected covering the central pit. Although the pit may have been constructed for a

Photograph of the Gore Mound before excavations. *Courtesy of the Grave Creek Archaeological Complex, West Virginia Department of Arts, Culture and History.*

Montgomery Incised pottery vessel from the Gore Mound. *Courtesy of the Grave Creek Mound Archaeological Complex, West Virginia Department of Arts, Culture and History.*

burial, no evidence of human remains was found.[122] The central tomb was given the designation Burial 2. The pit extended into subsoil and may have contained an extended adult burial.[123]

The excavation was expanded, and the cremated remains of two individuals were found at different locations approximately five feet from the central pit. Burial 1 consisted of 956 grams of small bone fragments. The condition of the bones was consistent with cremation, although no evidence of a crematory basin was found, suggesting the burial was cremated elsewhere.[124]

Associated with Burial 1 were the crushed remains of a Montgomery Incised pottery vessel. The pottery vessel was the only culturally deposited item found in the mound except for four tiny chert flakes found in the mound fill. Only about two-thirds of the vessel were recovered. Because of its close association with Burial 1, the vessel might have been used to transport the cremated remains to the mound site.[125]

About five feet north of Burial 1 was Burial 3, which consisted of twenty-one grams of burned bone covering an area measuring five and a half feet by two and a half feet. No artifacts were found with Burial 3, and no preparation of the area was observed.[126]

The Montgomery Incised pottery vessel was a jar with a rounded base and slightly everted rim. It was siltstone tempered and smoothed on the exterior and interior surfaces. Decoration was a series of very distinctive concentric diamonds incised into the exterior surface.[127]

Montgomery Incised vessels have been typically considered Late Adena. Several Montgomery Incised pottery vessels have been found in mounds and earthworks in Indiana, Ohio and Kentucky. A Montgomery Incised pottery vessel with similar surface treatments was found at the Morgan Stone Mound in Bath County, Kentucky, that was dated to 150 BC $\pm$ 150 years. Others date from 60 BC to AD 210 $\pm$ 140 years.[128]

GRAVE CREEK MOUND (46MR001)
AND SURROUNDING AREA

Few archaeological sites have inspired as much curiosity and speculation as the Grave Creek Mound in Moundsville, West Virginia. At 62 feet high and 240 feet in diameter, it remains the largest known conical burial mound in North America. Mound construction is thought to have taken fifty-seven thousand tons of earth, or approximately three million basket loads.[129] Originally, the Grave Creek Mound was a symmetrical cone and the top was surrounded by a parapet approximately 3 feet wide. The mound was also surrounded by a ditch or moat that was crossed by two passageways [130]

The Grave Creek Mound was located on Moundsville Bottom, which was also known as Grave Creek Flats and was a center of Adena activity in the Upper Ohio Valley. Moundsville Bottom contained approximately two thousand acres surrounded by hills.[131]

There were many other mounds in the area. Early accounts mentioned two small mounds about fifty yards from the Grave Creek Mound and a "small ditched circle with two entrances and a smaller ditched mound." Another early account described "four or five small mounds within a few hundred yards…of the big mound, each about 30 feet in diameter much lower in proportion and all rounded over the tops."[132]

In 1785, General Richard Butler described the earthworks near the great mound as follows:

> There are two small forts which, with the Grave, form a triangle. Near one of these forts are three large holes, which appear to me to have been places of deposit for provisions. About one fourth of a mile from these, forming an angle of about 25 degrees, is a large fort which the owner of the land has begun to plow up, where they find pieces of earthen kettles.[133]

Grave Creek Flats was first settled in 1771 by the Tomlinson family. Located on what was once known as the Flats of Grave Creek, the mound, also known as the Mammoth Mound, was discovered by Joseph Tomlinson, thought to be the Moundsville's earliest European settler, who moved to the area several years before the Revolutionary War. While hunting deer one day, he came across the mound.[134]

In 1803, Meriwether Lewis, of Lewis and Clark fame, visited the mound known as the "Big Grave" and noted "traces of old entrenchments" that were visible but were "so imperfect that they cannot be traced…for this enquire I had not leasure."[135]

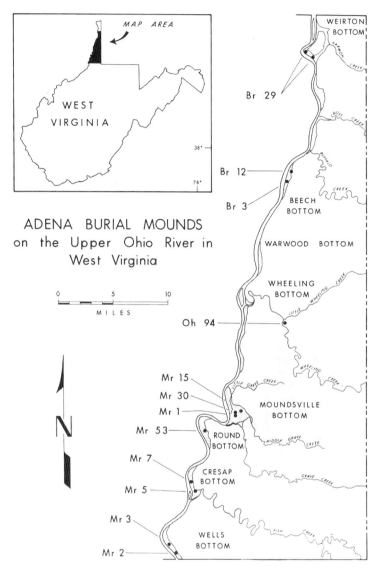

Map of Upper Ohio Valley in West Virginia showing locations of mound sites. *West Virginia Archeological Society, Hemmings, "Investigations at Grave Creek Mound."*

It appears that the outlines of the larger "fort" were still visible for years and might be the structure described in an 1876 newspaper article of the writer's memories of the 1838 period: "The fort contained, as I remember, about five acres, was an exact octagon, with bastions at the angles, and evidently by a skilled engineer, for defense."[136]

There were three smaller mounds near the large octagonal fort. The location of one is known and was on property owned by Colonel Joseph Biggs in the early 1800s.[137]

The mounds were known as graves by the first settlers to the area, and two local streams flowing into the Ohio River were known as Big Grave Creek and Little Grave Creek. The city of Moundsville was built between these two creeks. The area was first called the Flats of Grave Creek. Elizabeth Town was established at the northern end of the Flats that included most of the prehistoric mounds, including Grave Creek (Mammoth Mound), and Moundsville was established south of Elizabethtown. The two towns were consolidated after the Civil War to form the city of Moundsville.[138]

East of Grave Creek Mound, other mounds and earthworks dotted the landscape closer to the hills. These have all been demolished. It is thought that many of the earthworks were linked together with causeways or roads leading to the Ohio River and toward the hills to the east. The path toward the east was known as Red-Stone Old Fort during the colonial days, and it was near Brownsville, Pennsylvania. On his trip down the Ohio River in 1770, George Washington wrote in his diary, "At which place is a path leading to the settlement at Red Stone."[139]

In 1843, American anthropologist Henry Rowe Schoolcraft visited the Grave Creek Mound and created a map of the Grave Creek earthworks that was published in 1851. However, the earthworks were mostly obliterated by then, and the only structure that remained for any length of time was the Grave Creek Mound. Schoolcraft's map is the only authentic record of the Grave Creek earthworks that remains.[140]

According to Schoolcraft's map, there were seven mounds near the Grave Creek Mound that he had examined. These other mounds included:

1. The Elizabethtown Mound Group (46MR030), about 0.25 mile north of the Grave Creek Mound, that included three smaller mounds. When Schoolcraft visited in 1843, the mounds had been excavated for half a century. Found in one mound were Adena blocked-end cylindrical pipes, copper beads and a tablet.[141]

VIEW OF GRAVE CREEK MOUND.

Plate 1. View of Grave Creek Mound, from <u>Cincinnati Chronicle</u>, Feb. 2, 1939. A and B indicate tunnels into mound.

Illustration of Grave Creek Mound from *Cincinnati Chronicle*, February 2, 1939. A and B are tunnels into the mound. *Courtesy of the Grave Creek Mound Archaeological Complex, West Virginia Department of Arts, Culture and History.*

2. The Sheperd Mound (46MR15) was about one mile northeast of the Grave Creek Mound and had been excavated but was largely intact. Schoolcraft recorded an engraved Adena tablet from the mound known as the Grave Creek Sheperd Tablet. The whereabouts of the tablet have been long unknown.[142]

3. In addition to the above mounds, Schoolcraft recorded traces of three circular enclosures north and northeast of the Elizabethtown Group thought to be approximately three hundred to five hundred feet in diameter.[143]

4. Several early historic accounts by General Richard Butler in 1785, Major Jonathan Heart in 1791 and Thomas Nuttall in 1821 described square enclosures, straight embankments and scattered mounds. After moving to Ohio, a Mr. J.E. Wharton described a structure that was a perfect octagon.[144]

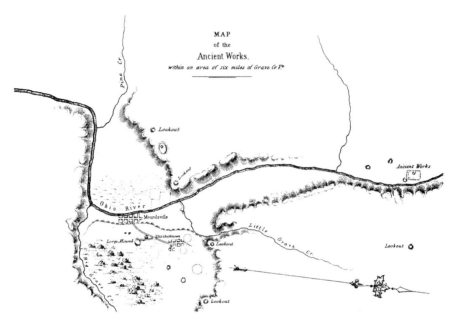

Early Schoolcraft map of ancient works near Moundsville, West Virginia. *Courtesy of the Grave Creek Mound Archaeological Complex, West Virginia Department of Arts, Culture and History.*

The earliest known photograph of the Grave Creek Mound, circa 1890–1910. *Courtesy of the Grave Creek Mound Archaeological Complex, West Virginia Department of Arts, Culture and History.*

For years, there were fanciful accounts of the mound and its contents. An early writer stated that the mound had been opened far enough to ascertain that it contained many thousands of human skeletons of "uncommon large size."[145]

Throughout his lifetime, Joseph Tomlinson, who owned the property on which the mound was located, refused to allow any excavations. However, at some point, a twelve-foot-long horizontal tunnel was drilled into the mound about halfway up the side. Part of a human jawbone was found, "the bone rough and honeycombed but the teeth entire and the surrounding clay of a white chalkey consistence." Joseph Tomlinson died around 1826.[146]

In 1838, a Moundsville newspaper published a letter from a H.E.D. & Co. that stated:

> Our negligence with regard to the excavation of our MAMMOTH MOUND, has called down the censure and reprobation of the enlightened of every community wherever the knowledge of the "Great Mound at Grave Creek" existed. Long has the scientific world gazed with an eager eye for its excavation.
>
> Where is the man who could say that our huge Monumental Mound, may not contain relics which will establish it beyond doubt, one of the first wonders of the world! Men, illustrious for their scientific and philosophical researches, have given it as their belief that it is the repository of some mighty race who preceded the supposed aborigines of this country, and that it is a sepulcher in which sleep some of the mighty rulers of the earth.
>
> Awake! awake! then citizens. Let us rally our full force. Roll in your mite, the undertaking is pregnant with the most glorious results! The minerals of Europe will be poured into our place in copious torrents.[147]

For a while, Joseph's son Jesse refused to permit the mound to be opened. However, after much pressure from the local community to excavate, in 1838, Tomlinson finally yielded and allowed excavation under the direction of his nephew Abelard Tomlinson and Thomas Biggs, Abelard's brother-in-law. By this time, they were convinced that the mound contained treasures.[148]

In 1838, road engineers measured the mound as 69 feet high and 295 feet in diameter at the base. The flat top of the mound measured 60 feet in diameter. The shape of the mound was a symmetrical cone, and it was surrounded by a ditch or moat with two passages across.[149]

Excavation of the mound began on Monday, March 19, 1838. The plan was "to commence an excavation at the level of the ground and after pushing it to the center to sink a shaft from the top to meet it. They would then arch and wall both with brick, build a staircase up the middle and establish a gentle 'toll' upon the curious who should desire to perambulate a sepulchre on bygone worthies whose slumbers had been for ages undisturbed."[150]

They chose a spot east of due north and four feet up the side of the mound to begin excavations. After a couple of days and ten to twelve feet of horizontal digging, the original ground surface appeared at an angle of about fifteen degrees. When they reached the center of the mound, they discovered that it had been built on a natural "rise" approximately seven or eight feet above the surrounding ground surface.[151]

The original ground surface was covered with a layer of bluish earth between one and one and a half inches thick. There were also "blue bunches" of soil in an oval shape that contained bits of charcoal and burned bone. It appeared that the original builders had used baskets full of earth from the surrounding area to construct the mound. Individual loads of soil from the surrounding area could be seen.[152]

After more digging, the excavators noticed a "covered passageway" leading downward ten to fifteen degrees to the base of the vault. The passageway had originally been covered with timber, and the impressions of the bark were still visible. The passageway had been partially filled up by fallen timbers and earth. From the impressions, the timbers were originally four to five inches in diameter.[153]

After a few more weeks of digging, the excavators encountered a "burial vault" approximately 111 feet from the point where they began their excavations and 7 or 8 feet below the natural ground surface. The vault was rectangular and approximately 8 by 12 feet in size. Logs had been placed upright to support the sides of the vault and "covered with a quantity of stones to the depth of two and a half feet."[154]

Inside the vault were the remains of two individuals, a male and a female, their heads near each other and their feet in opposite directions. The male was reported to be approximately five feet nine inches tall.[155] Dr. Townsend, a prominent surgeon in Wheeling, examined the bodies and estimated from the condition of their teeth that they were elderly at the time of death.[156]

The male individual was surrounded by 650 "ivory" beads. Dr. James Clemens reported that they were ivory and were probably cut from the tusks of mastodons. However, a few years later, Henry Schoolcraft, who was an ethnologist, determined that the beads were made from marine shell.[157]

Another item found with the male individual was what appears to be a large stone gorget that Delf Norona described many years later as an atlatl weight. There were no items found with the female individual.[158]

A ten-foot shaft was to be dug from the top of the mound downward. However, a large oak tree on top of the mound had to be removed. Within three feet of the top of the mound, the remains of several other individuals were encountered. These were thought to be intrusive burials of Native Americans from a later culture.[159]

The excavators used iron rods to probe downward, and about halfway, they met an obstruction. The probe had evidently struck a rock that fell in with a sound heard by the excavators and indicated another vault. They returned to the lower vault and probed upward to locate the upper vault. With the location of the upper vault in mind, the excavators began digging another horizontal tunnel outside and up the side of the mound about thirty-four feet. The upper vault was discovered on June 9. It was also full of earth, rotted wood and stones where the ceiling had fallen in. The upper vault was approximately eighteen by eighteen feet.[160]

The remains of one individual were inside the vault. The bones were very decayed, except for the teeth. There were 1,700 "ivory" beads, 500 "sea shells" worn as beads, a gorget, 5 copper bracelets on the wrists of the individual and a number of square or rectangular pieces of mica.

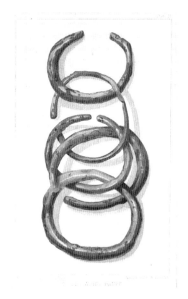

Illustration of copper bracelets from the Grave Creek Mound. *Courtesy of the Grave Creek Mound Archaeological Complex, West Virginia Department of Arts, Culture and History.*

The pieces of mica were from one and a half to two inches square with two or three holes. These were found all over the individual, and it was thought by the excavators that they had been strung together and worn as an ornament. A six-inch-long, flat diamond-shaped gorget was also found in the upper vault. In addition, the small flat inscribed Grave Creek stone or tablet was reportedly found there.[161]

The five hundred marine shell beads were around the neck and chest of the individual as a necklace. They were described by Dr. Clemens as "Oliva," but Schoolcraft wrote that they were "all of one species, the *Marginella flairda*."[162]

The excavations at the Grave Creek Mound in 1838 were the first recorded investigations of an Adena mound.[163]

A month after the excavations were completed, Jesse Tomlinson gave a thirty-year lease to his brother, Samuel; Samuel's son Abelard; and Samuel's son-in-law, Thomas Biggs. They would open the mound and its contents to the public. The men had plans to brick the lower tunnel and "build a staircase up the middle and establish a gentle 'toll' upon the curious."[164]

Jesse Tomlinson passed away before the mound was ready for public viewing, but Abelard continued with the plan. The sides of the tunnel were bricked, ending with a "Gothic arch." The lower burial vault was enlarged from eight by ten square feet to twenty-eight feet in diameter and nine feet high. It was then converted into a museum. During this work, the remains of ten more individuals were found in sitting positions in a very poor state of preservation.[165]

On top of the mound directly over the rotunda, a three-story building was constructed that was called an observatory. From the building, visitors had an excellent view of the surrounding country.[166]

A visitor to the mound museum related that the foundation of the shaft leading to the top of the mound was in the center of the museum, and around the perimeter were "departments" for "relics." A skeleton was fastened to the shaft leading to the top and was protected by a wire screen. The museum was lit by twenty candles.[167]

The museum was opened in May 1839, and the admission price was twenty-five cents and half price for children. However, because there were not enough tourists visiting, the museum was unsuccessful. It was abandoned around 1846. By one account, "the excavation proved to be pecuniarily, a bad operation. The rotunda has fallen in, the bolts and bars have vanished, and the gate to the enclosure no longer requires the incantation of a dime to crack a rusty welcome to the curious visitor."[168]

The mound museum was abandoned around 1847, and the property fell into disarray. The mound museum rotunda had fallen in and the gate to the fence was left unlocked, and animals and people came and went. In 1860, it was reported that the building on top of the mound had been replaced by a saloon.[169]

The property containing the mound changed ownership several times. At one time, the property was used as a county fairground with a racecourse around the mound. During the Civil War, artillery was stationed on top of the mound.[170]

After several ownership changes, and sales of much of the original twenty-one-acre parcel of land, the remaining one and three-quarter acres containing the mound was sold in 1874 to George S. McFadden, one-time warden of the nearby West Virginia Penitentiary. A couple of years later, McFadden wrote that "the board of directors of the West Virginia Penitentiary talk of purchasing the mound for the purpose of putting a basin on the top to supply the prison with water. The property should really belong to the state and be beautified for a pleasure ground."[171]

After McFadden's death in 1906, his son R.J. McFadden planned to destroy the mound. Local residents started a movement to raise money to purchase the mound. However, McFadden (the son), who had been persuaded to postpone the destruction of the mound while other solutions could be sought, decided to begin demolition of the mound on June 1, 1908.[172]

Fortunately, the Daughters of the American Revolution secured an option for one year to purchase the property for $20,000. Their hope was to postpone the date of the mound's destruction until some agency could come forward with the necessary funds. At the same time, the West Virginia superintendent of schools, Thomas C. Miller, contacted school personnel throughout the state soliciting ideas and ways to raise funds to help purchase the mound property. He announced November 5 as Mound Day and requested students throughout the state to make contributions toward the purchase of the property.[173]

Governor M.O. Dawson commented, "We do not expect the teachers and children to contribute all the money, but if they become interested in the matter…the money will be raised [by the state] and the mound will be preserved." At the end of Mound Day, about $1,400 had been raised by schools and various cities throughout the state.[174]

As promised by Governor Dawson, he gave his blessing to a bill in the legislature. House Bill 333 was passed on February 26, 1909, appropriating the additional $18,600 for the purchase of the mound property. The act also provided that the mound "shall be hereafter under the control of the Penitentiary Board and under the immediate supervision of the warden thereof."[175]

For several years, nothing was done to the mound. Finally, in 1915, warden M.Z. White filled in gullies and little caves and tunnels dug into the mound by children. The top depression was filled in, and grass seed, fertilizer and many tons of dirt were added. Shrubbery was also planted around the grounds.[176]

In 1952, the Mound Museum was opened, largely through the efforts of Delf Norona and the WVAS. In 1966, the Grave Creek Mound became a National Historic Landmark. In 1967, the property became the Grave Creek Mound State Park, and the Delf Norona Museum was opened to the public in 1978.[177] Now under the control of the West Virginia Department of Arts, Culture and History, the Grave Creek Mound and museum remains the state's preeminent center for history, archaeology and research.

The Moat

Between 1788 and 1839, some historical accounts from visitors to the Grave Creek Mound commented on the "ditch" around the mound. However, little has been written about this feature in the literature. One account in the journal of Captain Meriwether Lewis on September 9, 1803, said, "Around the base [of the Grave Creek Mound] runs a ditch 60 feet in width which is broken or intersected by a ledge of earth raised as high as the outer bank of the ditch—on the N.W. side, this bank is about 30 feet wide and appears to have formed the entrance to fortifyed the mound"[178] Because the ditch or moat was not mentioned in the literature after 1840, it may have been filled to the surrounding ground level between 1818 and 1839.[179]

In 1975 and 1976, several archaeological investigations were conducted at the Grave Creek Mound. This was the first systematic archaeological work at the mound and the first excavations since the early excavations in

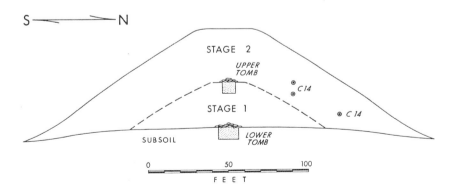

Cross section of the Grave Creek Mound showing locations of tombs and core samples for C14 dating. *West Virginia Archeological Society, Hemmings, "Investigations at Grave Creek Mound."*

Grave Creek Mound today. *Courtesy of the Grave Creek Mound Archaeological Complex, West Virginia Department of Arts, Culture and History.*

1838.[180] The projects were conducted by the West Virginia Geological and Economic Survey through an agreement with the West Virginia Department of Natural Resources.[181] At that time, the mound was approximately 62 feet (19 meters) high, and the diameter of the mound was 240 feet (73 meters). The excavators used exploratory trenching at the edge of the mound to locate the moat that had surrounded it. The moat was about 910 feet long at the centerline, 40 feet wide and 4 to 5 feet deep.[182]

Core drilling was used at the mound as a means to study the interior without excavation. Samples from the core drilling returned a radiocarbon date of 200 BC.[183]

The Grave Creek Tablet

Perhaps the most controversial object possibly from the Grave Creek Mound is the Grave Creek Tablet. The stone or tablet is a small sandstone piece about one and a half by two inches in size. Its whereabouts today are unknown.[184]

In the early nineteenth century, there were historians who were looking for proof that Europeans had first inhabited America. The Grave Creek Tablet was thought by some to possibly represent a Runic writing of the

The Grave Creek Tablet
(Drawn from the original by Capt. Seth Eastman in 1850)

The Grave Creek Tablet. *Courtesy of the Grave Creek Mound Archaeological Complex, West Virginia Department of Arts, Culture and History.*

Norsemen or some other European language that had been placed in the upper burial vault during ancient times.[185]

To make things more confusing, there were various accounts at the time of who had found the Grave Creek Tablet and where it had been found. There were several "translations" made in various languages. However, the current thinking among archaeologists is that the Grave Creek Tablet was a hoax.[186]

HALF MOON SITE (46BR029)

The Half Moon Site included a group of four mounds located along the Ohio River near Weirton in Brooke County, West Virginia. The site was located on approximately five hundred acres of bottomland on the Patterson farm. One of the mounds was approximately forty-four feet in diameter and thirty inches high. The largest mound was sixty feet in diameter and six feet high. There were several pits dug into the mound. The remaining two mounds had been leveled before development.[187]

In 1940, Elmer W. Fetzer with the WVAS excavated one of the mounds known as Mound No. 1. Near the center of the mound was a subfloor pit containing the remains of an individual in an extended position. On the chest of the individual were 252 rolled copper beads.[188] Over the burial was a small mound of dark earth and a layer of ash. Above this was

Photograph of the Half Moon Mound before excavation. *Courtesy of the Grave Creek Mound Archaeological Complex, West Virginia Department of Arts, Culture and History.*

another thick layer of earth containing a bundle burial and fragments of bone.[189]

A leaf-shaped blade and approximately one quart of red ocher was found near floor level. Items found in the mound fill included a fragment of a banded slate gorget, two broken celts, several notched and stemmed blades and several pieces of chert thought to be scrapers. On the ground surface near the mound were fragments of gorgets, hematite hemispheres and blocked-end tubular pipes.[190]

On a second terrace of the Ohio River and approximately five hundred feet south of Mound No. 1 was a slightly elevated area. There was some speculation about the area and whether it was natural or possibly a man-made mound. The area had been cultivated for over a century.[191]

In 1944, Elmer Fetzer and Walter Singer of Wellsburg decided to trench a section of the mound known as Mound No. 3. They cut a five-foot trench toward the center of the mound, where they encountered rocks of various sizes. As they widened the trench, they noted that the rocks were placed in a circle approximately six feet wide and eighteen inches thick surrounding a three-foot interior. The inside of the stone circle contained a "bushel" of charcoal.[192] The earth outside the stone circle was darker and softer except for the north side. When the excavators

Top: Broken slate gorget from the Half Moon Site. *Courtesy of the Grave Creek Mound Archaeological Complex, West Virginia Department of Arts, Culture and History.*

Middle: Stone gorget from the Half Moon Site. *Courtesy of the Grave Creek Mound Archaeological Complex, West Virginia Department of Arts, Culture and History.*

Bottom: Assorted bifaces from the Half Moon Mound. *Courtesy of the Grave Creek Mound Archaeological Complex, West Virginia Department of Arts, Culture and History.*

Top: Stone axe from the Half Moon Site. *Courtesy of the Grave Creek Mound Archaeological Complex, West Virginia Department of Arts, Culture and History.*

Middle: Adena leaf-shaped bifaces from the Half Moon Site. *Courtesy of the Grave Creek Mound Archaeological Complex, West Virginia Department of Arts, Culture and History.*

Bottom: Biface from the Half Moon Site. *Courtesy of the Grave Creek Mound Archaeological Complex, West Virginia Department of Arts, Culture and History.*

Top: Grit-tempered pottery sherds from the Half Moon Site. *Courtesy of the Grave Creek Mound Archaeological Complex, West Virginia Department of Arts, Culture and History.*

Bottom: Chert scraper from the Half Moon Site. *Courtesy of the Grave Creek Mound Archaeological Complex, West Virginia Department of Arts, Culture and History.*

removed the disturbed area, they found a second floor lower than the first one. Nothing of interest was found.[193]

Pottery from the Half Moon Site included many Fayette Thick sherds, also called Half Moon cordmarked by Mayer-Oakes.[194]

HYER (HYRE) MOUND (46RD001)

The Hyer Mound, also known as the Hyre Mound, was located in Randolph County, West Virginia, on a low ridge in the upper Tygart Valley. According to Bettye Broyles, who excavated the mound in 1963 for the West Virginia Geological and Economic Survey, the mound was constructed of stone and sandy clay. At the time of excavation, the mound was forty by forty-four feet in diameter and nearly five feet high. Broyles reported a Middle Woodland mound and village located on a terrace about thirty feet above the valley floor between Elkwater Fork and the Tygart Valley River.[195]

Forty ten-foot squares were excavated at the village site. Several cooking pits were found, described as holes dug into the ground and lined with stones. The pits contained broken pottery and charcoal. No house patterns were observed at the village site. Artifacts recovered from the mound and village included clay-tempered Armstrong Plain pottery, projectile points, drills, scrapers, hammerstones and fragments of celts. Nutting stones were found only in the mound.[196]

Twenty burials were removed from the mound, which was totally excavated. One individual found beneath the mound had been cremated. Other individuals had been buried intact, and sixteen were bundle burials.[197]

No artifacts were found with the burials. Seven of the individuals were partially covered with large stones. Other items found in the mound included two rolled copper beads, a large cache of blades made from Flint Ridge chert and an Armstrong cordmarked pottery vessel. A piece of a stone tubular pipe and a clay elbow pipe were also found.[198]

KANAWHA VALLEY MOUND COMPLEX

According to early Adena researchers William Webb and Charles Snow, who wrote *The Adena People* in 1945, there were several areas in the Ohio Valley where Adena occupation was particularly concentrated. One of those areas was the Kanawha Valley of West Virginia near Charleston (see map).

During the archaeological investigations by Cyrus Thomas for the Bureau of Ethnology of the Smithsonian Institution in the 1880s, several mounds in West Virginia were excavated. Colonel P.W. Norris supervised the investigations in West Virginia. The explorations in West Virginia were mainly on the Kanawha River and its tributaries. This was the first systematic investigation of these structures. In his notes, Thomas called the large mound complex between Charleston and Dunbar the "Ancient City of Kanawha." He described the "Ancient Works Near Charleston" as "the most extensive and interesting ancient works to be found in the state of West Virginia."[199]

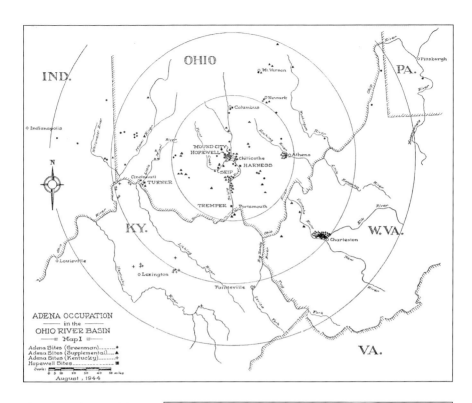

Above: Map from Webb and Snow (1945) showing areas of Adena occupation, including the Kanawha Valley near Charleston, West Virginia. *Courtesy of the William S. Webb Museum of Anthropology, University of Kentucky.*

Right: Map of Kanawha County mounds from Thomas (1887, Plate V). *West Virginia Archeological Society, Youse, "Excavation of the Young Mound."*

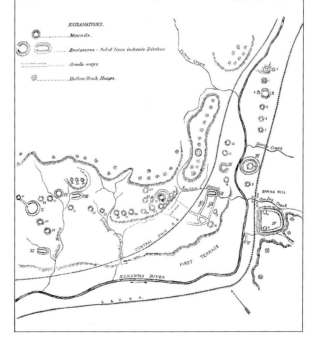

Thomas reported fifty earthen mounds, extensive earthworks and eight to ten enclosures. All were located on upper terraces of the Kanawha River.[200] Today, after years of farming and development, only a handful of the earthen mounds remain. None of the earthworks is known to exist.

Creel Mound (No. 1)

Mound No. 1 on Thomas's map and one of the most well-known and largest remaining mounds in the Kanawha Valley is the Creel Mound, also known as the South Charleston Mound. The Creel Mound is listed in the National Register of Historic Places and in West Virginia is second in size only to the Grave Creek Mound. The mound was on property owned by the Creel family. Sometime between the Smithsonian excavations and publication of the volume by Thomas, the family name was misspelled as "Criel," and it has been misspelled in the literature since then.

The Creel Mound is located in the city of South Charleston along U.S. Route 60. At the time of the Smithsonian excavations, the Creel family gave permission to Colonel Norris to excavate the mound as long as their representative could be present and all the "gold, diamonds and silver" found would be theirs.[201]

Aerial photograph of the Creel (or South Charleston) Mound. *Courtesy of the U.S. Army Corps of Engineers, Huntington District.*

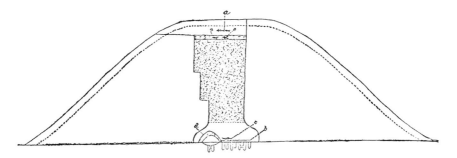

Cross section of the Creel Mound. *Thomas,* Report on the Mound Explorations.

The excavation of the Creel Mound began in 1883. At that time, the top of the mound had been leveled to accommodate a judge's stand for a racetrack that circled the mound. The remaining mound stood 33 feet high and 520 feet in circumference. A 12-foot shaft was sunk through the center of the mound to the original surface of the ground. At a depth of 3 feet, human bone was found, thought to be the remains of an individual reportedly dug up with the construction of the judge's stand. At 4 feet, two burials were encountered in a matrix of mixed clay and ash. The individuals were lying extended on their backs with their heads to the south and their feet toward the center of the mound. Found with these individuals were two celts, two stone hoes, one projectile point and two stone disks.[202]

At twenty-four feet, the soil changed, and there were decayed fragments of logs up to twelve inches in diameter. At thirty-one feet from the top, a human skeleton lay with head to the north and fragments of copper thought by Thomas to have been a headdress. The shaft was enlarged to sixteen feet and the base of the mound uncovered, revealing a surface covered by elm bark. On top of the bark was a layer of fine white ashes. The individual had been placed on this prepared surface and covered with similar bark. Ten more burials were found at this depth, five arranged on each side in a semicircle, with heads outward and feet toward, but not touching, the individual in the center. Each burial on the east side had what appeared to be an unused projectile point. One of these five individuals also had what Thomas called a "fish dart," three "arrowheads" and mussel shells. Six shell beads and a "lance head" were found with the individual in the center.[203]

From the wood fragments and circular holes, thought to represent post molds, found on the natural surface, Colonel Norris concluded that these

Top: Copper sheets from the Creel Mound. *(Catalogue No. A90694) Department of Anthropology, Smithsonian Institution.*

Middle: Bifaces from the Creel Mound. *(Catalogue No. 90697) Department of Anthropology, Smithsonian Institution.*

Bottom: Olivella marine shell beads from the Creel Mound. *(Catalogue No. 90699) Department of Anthropology, Smithsonian Institution.*

Wood fragments from the structure beneath the Creel Mound. *(Catalogue No. 90696) Department of Anthropology, Smithsonian Institution.*

eleven individuals had probably been buried in a timber-walled structure approximately sixteen feet in diameter.[204]

Near the center of the mound was a clay vault approximately four feet deep and five feet in diameter. The vault had been dug into the natural ground surface and contained rotted wood, bark and bones, some of them human. There were two holes sixteen inches in diameter and four feet deep at the bottom of the vault. They were lined with bluish clay and partly filled with water. Similar pairs of holes were found besides the heads of each of the ten surrounding individuals.[205]

Wilson Mound (No. 8)

Mound No. 8 on Thomas's map, also known as the Wilson Mound, is still standing. The mound was originally within Enclosure C. According to Thomas, the square enclosure was five to six feet high and enclosed approximately twenty acres with a ditch inside the walls.[206]

The mound had been opened by the Wilson family years before the Smithsonian explorations, and the enclosure had been leveled. Near the center of the mound, human bone and several celts and "lance heads" had been found. At the time of the Smithsonian excavations, the mound was being used as a cemetery.[207] The Wilson Mound has continued to be used as a cemetery until recently.

Great Smith Mound (No. 21)

Across the Kanawha River in the city of Dunbar, a group of mounds was located on a high terrace that is now a residential neighborhood. In 1969, Hillis Youse, a member of the WVAS, attempted to locate the remnants of this group of mounds. Using old deed books and maps and interviewing longtime residents of Dunbar, Youse was able to determine the locations of twelve of the mounds documented by the Smithsonian in the 1880s.[208]

At the time of the Smithsonian excavations, many of the mounds were located on the 780-acre farm of Benjamin H. Smith. The largest of the group, Mound No. 21, also known as the Great Smith Mound, was 175 feet in diameter and 35 feet high at the time of the excavations.[209]

In the top of the mound were the remains of an individual in a stone slab coffin thought to be a later, intrusive burial. A twelve-foot diameter shaft was sunk through the top of the mound. At the depth of six feet, skeletal remains were found that were described by Thomas as a bundle burial.[210]

At nine feet below the top of the mound, another burial was found within the remains of a black walnut coffin. At fourteen feet, a large individual was found in an upright position with his back against a hard clay wall. Around the skeleton were the remains of a bark wrapping. Two copper bracelets were on his left wrist.[211]

At this point, the excavators had entered the remains of a large wooden burial vault. The top had collapsed. Nineteen feet from the top of the mound,

Copper bracelets from the Great Smith Mound. *(Catalogue No. A90738) Department of Anthropology, Smithsonian Institution.*

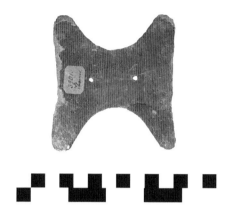

Top: Copper gorget from the Great Smith Mound. *(Catalogue No. A88014) Department of Anthropology, Smithsonian Institution.*

Bottom: Marginella shell beads from the Great Smith Mound. *(Catalogue No. 90747) Department of Anthropology, Smithsonian Institution.*

they encountered the bottom of the vault where a very large individual was found in the remains of a bark coffin. According to Thomas, the skeleton measured seven and a half feet long and nineteen inches across the shoulders. There were six copper bracelets on each wrist and a copper gorget upon the chest. Several flint bifaces and hematite tools were found, as well as a large number of small perforated marine shells and thirty-two shell beads. Upon the left shoulder of the individual were three large sheets of mica.[212]

The log vault was nearly square and measured thirteen by twelve feet inside. Also inside the vault were the remains of four adults, one in each corner placed in a leaning position against the sides of the vault. They had been wrapped in bark and were found with several bifaces described as "lance heads and fish darts" and a few shell beads.[213]

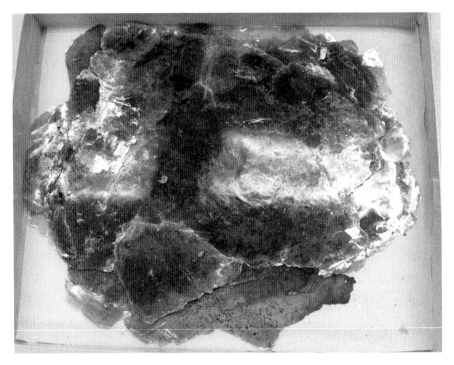

Mica sheets from the Great Smith Mound. *(Catalogue No. 90740) Department of Anthropology, Smithsonian Institution.*

Mound No. 21 appears to have been constructed in several stages. Below the floor of the log vault there were several feet of mottled dark clay, and below that lay a heavy layer of ashes, charcoal and charred bones, some of them human. This is probably evidence of human cremations before the actual mound construction.

The large wooden burial vault with five burials probably represents the second stage of construction, that of the actual mound and possibly the burial of an honored leader whose death initiated the mound-building sequence. Other burials were placed above the wooden vault over time. And finally, perhaps many years later, it appears that a member of a later population was buried in the top of the mound.

Mound No. 22 was located southeast of No. 21 and was one hundred feet in diameter and fifteen feet high. A trench was dug across it to the center and down to the original ground surface. The top two feet was loose soil. Below that was a layer of hard gray soil four feet thick with an area in the center eight feet in diameter and ten inches thick containing decayed charcoal, ash and bone. In the center of the mound twelve feet from the top were the

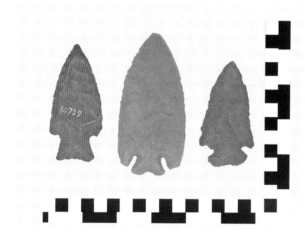

Top: Hematite hemisphere from the Great Smith Mound. *(Catalogue No. 90730) Department of Anthropology, Smithsonian Institution.*

Middle: Assorted bifaces from the Great Smith Mound. *(Catalogue Nos. A90739 and A88001) Department of Anthropology, Smithsonian Institution.*

Bottom: Adena bifaces from the Great Smith Mound. *(Catalogue No. 90739) Department of Anthropology, Smithsonian Institution.*

Top: Stone celts from the Great Smith Mound. *(Catalogue Nos. 90720, 90721 and 90723a) Department of Anthropology, Smithsonian Institution.*

Middle: Stone platform pipe from the Great Smith Mound. *(Catalogue No. 90840) Department of Anthropology, Smithsonian Institution.*

Bottom: Clay pipe from the Smith farm. *(Catalogue No. A88021) Department of Anthropology, Smithsonian Institution.*

Top: Snyders biface from the Smith farm. *(Catalogue No. 87952) Department of Anthropology, Smithsonian Institution.*

Middle: Slate pendant from the Smith farm. *(Catalogue No. 88025) Department of Anthropology, Smithsonian Institution.*

Bottom: Chert bladelets from the Smith farm. *(Catalogue No. A88018) Department of Anthropology, Smithsonian Institution.*

remains of an individual in a horizontal position with its head to the south. A slender copper bracelet was on the left wrist, and there were two spear heads close.[214]

Catacomb Mound (No. 23)

Mound No. 23 was also on the Smith farm. It was called the Catacomb Mound because of a series of "circular oven-like" or "beehive-shaped vaults" in a semicircle at the bottom of the mound. The vaults were dry and contained dust and vegetable remains that Colonel Norris described as "maize in the ear" and a few bone fragments.[215]

The mound was located near the corner of Fletcher Avenue and Twentieth Street in Dunbar next to the Mound School.[216] The mound has been leveled over the years by school construction. At the time of the Smithsonian excavations, the mound was 312 feet in circumference and 25 feet high.[217] A large central shaft was sunk from the top of the mound. At approximately 15 feet, the casts of timbers and poles were uncovered extending into the sides of the mound. The wood remains continued for about 10 feet. Thomas described the remains as a circular wooden vault approximately 12 feet across and 8 to 10 feet high at the center. Two adult burials were found on the floor of the vault.[218]

The shaft was continued another four feet deep, revealing a pit sunken into the original ground surface and the semicircle of vaults. The bottom of the central pit was covered with several inches of ash and charcoal, suggesting it had held a fire. The excavations were halted at that time because of bad weather.[219]

Adena bifaces from the Catacomb Mound. *(Catalogue No. A113821) Department of Anthropology, Smithsonian Institution.*

Top: Stone gorgets and pendant from the Catacomb Mound. *(Catalogue No. A113782) Department of Anthropology, Smithsonian Institution.*

Bottom: Mussel shell from the Catacomb Mound. *(Catalogue No. A113797) Department of Anthropology, Smithsonian Institution.*

When Colonel Norris returned the next season, he dug trenches from the sides of the mound to the central shaft. One of the trenches nine feet from the top of the mound uncovered human bone but no complete remains. One half of the mound was then removed and examined. The fill dirt contained many broken stone tools and several mussel shells thought to have been used for digging.[220]

The continuing excavations revealed several more individual burials, one of which was in a stone slab coffin. All of these burials were below the natural ground surface.[221]

Young Mound 46KA065 (No. 30)

In 1967, members of the WVAS were given permission to excavate a mound in Dunbar that would be destroyed during the construction of a house.[222] The mound, designated No. 30 by Colonel Norris, had been opened by the Smithsonian during its investigations. At that time, the mound was twenty-one feet high and three hundred feet in circumference. The top of the mound contained a stone grave with what was thought to be an intrusive burial.[223]

A twelve-foot circular shaft was sunk into the top of the mound to the bottom, revealing only decayed wood and bark fragments that Thomas believed to be remnants of a wooden vault. The natural floor had been covered by bark and ashes. There was also a circle approximately twelve feet in diameter of vaults three feet wide by three feet high containing mud. The excavations were discontinued at that time because of water.[224]

By 1967, the mound had been leveled to about five feet high and disturbed by pothunting. However, excavations by the WVAS members located the remains of a log tomb on the mound floor apparently missed by the earlier excavations. The structure was approximately fifteen feet long (east–west) and ten

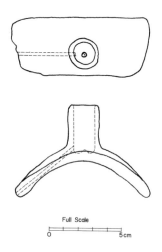

Drawing of platform pipe from the Young Mound. *West Virginia Archeological Society, Youse, "Excavation of the Young Mound."*

WOODLAND MOUNDS IN WEST VIRGINIA

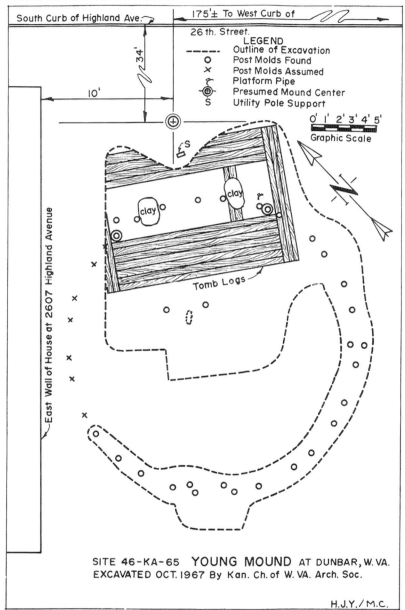

Plan map of the Young Mound excavations. Of interest is the circular pattern of paired post molds commonly found under Adena mounds. *West Virginia Archeological Society, Youse, "Excavation of the Young Mound."*

and a half feet wide (north–south) with inside dimensions about eleven by four feet. The side logs were laid three or four abreast on the north end and six or more abreast on the south and two or three at each end. Two post molds ten inches in diameter and nineteen inches deep were found in two inside corners of the structure. Fragments of wood resembling cedar were found in these post molds, as well as some of the log molds.[225]

Artifacts found during excavations included pieces of broken flint, cannel coal, hematite, a bone from a fawn and a platform pipe made from blue-grey limestone. No human remains were found, although there was some evidence that any burials might have been cremations.[226]

Artifacts from the mound fill such as small pottery sherds and Armstrong-type artifacts suggest a late date of construction. The platform pipe is similar to one found in Ohio that has been dated around 800 BC.[227]

The Young Mound has one calibrated radiocarbon date of 161 BC.[228]

Poorhouse Mound (No. 31)

Mound No. 31 was located on the Kanawha County Poor Farm. It still exists today in Institute, West Virginia, and is known as the Shawnee Reservation Mound. At the time of the Smithsonian excavation, the mound measured 318 feet in circumference, 25 feet high and 40 feet across the top. A 10-foot shaft was sunk from the top of the mound, and trenches were dug in from the sides. A layer of mixed clay and ash was discovered 3 feet below the top of the mound. Throughout the mound to the bottom, the soil was mixed with ashes.[229]

Three feet below the top of the mound were two extended individuals, one above the other, facing each other. Near the heads of the individuals were a pipe, a celt and several flint bifaces.[230]

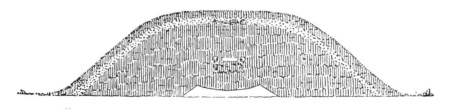

Cross section of the Poorhouse Farm or Shawnee Reservation Mound. *Thomas*, Report on the Mound Explorations.

Aerial photograph of the Poorhouse Farm or Shawnee Reservation Mound in Institute, West Virginia. *Courtesy of the U.S. Army Corps of Engineers, Huntington District, and Dr. Robert Maslowski.*

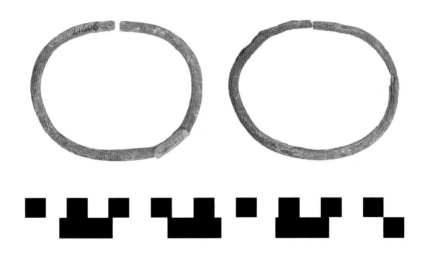

Copper bracelets from the Poorhouse Farm Mound. *(Catalogue No. A90717) Department of Anthropology, Smithsonian Institution.*

Ten feet below the top of the mound were two very large individuals facing each other in a sitting position with their legs interlocked to the knees. Above their outstretched hands was a large hollowed-out sandstone slab. The stone slab, which was two feet across, had been burned and was red and brittle. The hollowed cavity on the stone slab was filled with white ashes containing the fragments of burned bones. Over the slab was another slab of limestone three inches thick. Two copper bracelets were on the left wrist of one of the individuals. A hematite celt and "lancehead" was with the other.[231]

At twenty-five feet from the top of the mound, the excavators reached the natural ground surface. On top of the surface was a clay pad six to eighteen inches thick with a concave center that Thomas[232] described as an "altar." The upper portion of the clay pad had been burned to a deep red. The clay pad extended wider than the excavation shaft. On the top of the pad was a layer of fine white ashes from less than a foot to two feet thick. Intermingled with the ashes were stones that showed signs of heating and fragments of bones.[233]

Leslie Mound (46PU003)

The Leslie Mound and village sites are located on the southwest side of the Kanawha River in Scott District, Putnam County, West Virginia, approximately four miles upriver from Winfield. The mound site is on a "rolling bottomland with slight undulating ridges paralleling the Kanawha River. The Leslie Mound was about three hundred yards from the river's edge on the third ridge from the river. Scattered evidence of campsites is found on all the exposed ridges but is most heavily concentrated on the second ridge from the river."[234]

The property on which the mound was located was owned by Fred and John Leslie and was soon to be the site of a housing development, Shawnee Estates, which would destroy the mound. In 1962, Charles Butcher and Oscar Mairs discovered the mound was in danger of destruction. They talked with the Leslies and received permission to conduct a salvage excavation on the mound. The excavation was to be conducted by the Kanawha Chapter of the WVAS.[235]

Dr. Edward McMichael, archaeologist with the West Virginia Geological and Economic Survey, provided technical advice and was present while excavations were conducted. The Leslies allowed the Kanawha Chapter extra time than what was originally agreed upon to complete excavations.

They also provided mechanical equipment at the beginning of the project. The excavation began on Sunday, May 13, 1962, and took place each Sunday until June 10, 1962.[236]

A topographic survey was made of the mound and an arbitrary grid system put in place before excavations began. The mound appeared to be approximately one hundred feet in diameter and two and a half feet tall. It was thought to have been originally larger but had been previously reduced by cultivation.[237]

Using a backhoe, John Leslie cut across the center of the mound from east to west. The trench was approximately forty feet long, two feet wide and three feet deep. About two and a half feet below the current top of the mound, an old ground level was encountered. Beneath the mound, an old, thin humus occupation zone was observed. Several post molds were also uncovered, and charcoal samples were taken.[238]

After the first cut with the backhoe, a bulldozer excavated the south side of the mound nearly to ground level. Traces of a cremation burial were uncovered, and the bulldozer was stopped. Using shovels, more earth was removed from the south side of the mound in an area twenty by forty feet to a few inches from the base of the mound. The ground surface was cleaned, and a partial oval post mold was discovered. Next, the area between the backhoe trench and the bulldozed area was removed.[239]

The north side of the mound was then removed with the bulldozer to the bottom of the plow zone, and the remainder was removed using shovels. Another area about forty by twenty feet was removed to the ground surface. The east and west sides were cut down using a small bulldozer, and the final cut was through the center area below the mound.[240]

The mound consisted of slightly loamy clay similar to the subsoil. The mound fill was a bit lighter and the subsoil more yellow. There were occasional darker areas in the fill that were thought to represent basket loads of soil with a higher humus or debris content. The mound was separated from the subsoil by an occupational layer of humus that was darker brown and from one to four inches thick containing organic remains, charcoal flecks and bits of clay and rock.[241]

During the excavation, ten features were uncovered. The features included two cremation burials, several post molds thought to be part of a house pattern and several fire basins and oval pits.[242]

Many post molds found were thought to represent several superimposed house patterns. Some of the post molds appeared to slant outward, and some were set in pairs. Charred vegetal remains in some of the post molds included hickory nut fragments, acorn meats and shells and at least one sunflower seed. Two small granite celts were found in post molds with other rocks. Four pieces of Armstrong Plain clay-tempered pottery were found in another post mold.[243]

There was an area found in the center of the post molds where "intense burning" had taken place. This was thought to be from throwing earth over the remnants of the structure that might have been ceremonially burned. Armstrong Plain pottery sherds were found in the area, as well as a side-notched biface and a piece of rubbed hematite. Pieces of calcined bone, lumps of clay, some chert chips and a piece of mica schist were found on the old surface. Numerous artifacts were found in the mound fill.[244]

One radiocarbon date was obtained for the Leslie Mound of 300 BC.[245]

Murad Mound (46KA030)

The Murad Mound (46KA030) was located on a high terrace of the Kanawha River east of St. Albans in Kanawha County. The mound was in an urban area, and Oscar Mairs of the WVAS had been monitoring it for many years.[246]

In 1962, Andrew Murad, the owner of the property, decided to develop the area containing the mound. Mairs was informed of its impending destruction and contacted Dr. Edward McMichael, archaeologist with the West Virginia Geological and Economic Survey. Because the mound was to be impacted, an excavation was planned. Dr. McMichael began excavations on the mound in August 1962, with the removal of several large trees and underbrush. Next, the mound was measured, and a contour map was made. The mound dimensions measured seventy-eight feet east to west and ninety feet north to south. The flattened top of the mound was thirty feet east to west and forty feet north to south. The mound height at the time of excavation was ten and a half feet.[247]

Although the Murad Mound was relatively undisturbed, the excavators found evidence for one modern excavation.[248] Excavations began by hand using a shovel and mattock to break up the hard, compacted clay soil. Trowels were used when a burial was encountered.[249]

The first burial encountered was at the bottom of the north side of the mound. This was a large log tomb that contained one individual. Preservation

Photograph of the Murad Mound at the beginning of 1962 excavations. *Courtesy of the Grave Creek Mound Archaeological Complex, West Virginia Department of Arts, Culture and History.*

was very poor due to the penetration by tree rootlets, and all that remained were the teeth and right metacarpals and bones in the individual's right hand that had been preserved by contact with copper bracelets.[250]

The tomb was thought to have been constructed by first applying a layer of bluish-white clay, upon which the individual was placed extended on his back with his head toward the southeast. Next, logs were placed along each side and at the end of the burial. Post molds were found in each corner of the burial three to four inches in diameter and one on the south side. Additional logs had been placed on the first two, and a bark cover was placed over the entire tomb. Sandstone slabs were placed over the bark in the southwest corner.[251]

The individual was thought to be a male because it was relatively tall, although the pelvis and skull were missing.[252] Two C-shaped solid copper bracelets were found where the individual's wrists would have been. The individual measured six feet four inches and sixteen inches wide. However, it is assumed that the weight of the mound soil above the burial probably would have spread the skeletal remains. Measurements taken of the femur and tibia in situ suggest that the individual was probably five feet ten inches tall, although even these measurements could reflect spreading from the weight of the overlying earth.[253]

Copper bracelets from the Murad Mound. *Courtesy of the Grave Creek Mound Archaeological Complex, West Virginia Department of Arts, Culture and History.*

In 1963, work resumed on the Murad Mound supervised by Mairs. A second log tomb was discovered in the left side of the mound. With assistance from members of the WVAS, the second tomb was uncovered. This feature measured eighteen feet long by twelve feet nine inches wide and was approximately forty inches high. The bottom logs were ten to twelve inches thick and were placed two on a side and three across each end. Analyzed portions of the logs proved to be American red cedar or juniper. A sample was radiocarbon dated and returned a date of 100 BC ± 140.[254]

Inside the corners of the tomb were post molds six inches in diameter and twenty-nine inches deep. These suggested upright posts were used to support a covering over the burial. Inside the log enclosure was a prepared clay layer one to two inches thick, ten feet ten inches long and five feet seven inches wide. Upon the clay surface was a poorly preserved individual lying extended on his or her back with the head toward the east. The individual was estimated to be thirty to forty years of age from the amount of wear on its teeth.[255]

The individual measured six feet one inch in situ, although much spreading had occurred. By measuring the left femur and tibia, using a formula by Anderson,[256] an estimate of five feet six and a half inches was obtained. The individual's lower legs were covered with red ocher, and all was covered with bark. Under the head and feet was what looked like matting. Copper hollow rolled bracelets were on both wrists.

Once the excavations were complete, the mound was leveled. The mound appeared to have been constructed from the south side, with Tomb No. 1 constructed first.[257] Of the artifacts recovered from the Murad Mound, only the copper bracelets were found in situ. Other artifacts from the mound fill included chipped stone bifaces and tools, Armstrong Plain and Fayette

Thick pottery sherds, ground stone, calcined bone (some human), mussel shell and a walnut shell fragment.[258]

NATRIUM MOUND (46MR002)

The Natrium Mound was located in a field near the Pittsburgh Plate Glass Company approximately six miles down the Ohio River from the Cresap Mound in Marshall County, West Virginia. The Grave Creek Mound was a few miles north of the Natrium Mound. The Natrium Mound was on a tract of land called Wells Bottom that was originally part of a farm owned by the Arrick family.[259] The mound was twelve feet high and sixty-five feet in diameter at the base. The top of the mound had been dug into sometime in the past, and the south side was also disturbed.[260]

The Pittsburgh Plate Glass Company had planned to tear down the mound five years earlier. At that time, Joseph Essington wrote to the Smithsonian Institution's Bureau of Ethnology about the plans to destroy the mound. The glass company decided not to go forward at that time; however, three years later, it revived its plans.[261]

The Smithsonian began developing a plan for excavation of the mound with the cooperation of Pittsburgh Plate Glass Company. Excavations began on December 7, 1948, with Ralph Solecki from the Smithsonian Institution

Left: Popeyed birdstone from the Natrium Mound. *(Catalogue No. 398399-0) Department of Anthropology, Smithsonian Institution.*

Right: Stone axe from the Natrium Mound. *(Catalogue No. A398423) Department of Anthropology, Smithsonian Institution.*

Top: Three Adena bifaces from the Natrium Mound. *(Catalogue No. A398433) Department of Anthropology, Smithsonian Museum.*

Middle: Modified stone tubular pipe from the Natrium Mound. *(Catalogue No. A398378-0) Department of Anthropology, Smithsonian Institution.*

Bottom: Copper gorget with textile impressions from the Natrium Mound. *(Catalogue No. A398349-0) Department of Anthropology, Smithsonian Institution.*

supervising the project. Several future members of the WVAS volunteered on the excavation. These included Delf Norona Sr. and Delf Norona Jr., William and Robert Athey and Oscar Mairs.[262]

Once trees and bushes had been removed from the mound, a grid system of five-foot squares running north–south by east–west was placed over the mound and staked. Excavations of the Natrium Mound took place for twenty-three days, beginning in December 1948 and continuing until January 1949. Because time was critical, a bulldozer was used to remove the bulk of the soil. For more delicate work, wheelbarrows, trowels and shovels were used.[263]

Because the excavations took place in the winter, three canvas tarpaulins were tied onto wooden frames over the work area. In addition, a fire was kept going nearby. Temperatures were brutal and were frequently below freezing. One day, the temperature was fourteen degrees Fahrenheit. Nevertheless, the work continued every day.[264]

The top of the mound had been disturbed by previous digging.[265] Fifty-one features were found in the Natrium Mound, and twenty-two were burials. There were also several other features that the excavators thought had contained burials, but any remains that might have once been there were gone.[266]

The birdstone found at the Natrium Mound was the first one recorded for an Adena mound.[267] One burial, designated Burial Feature No. 34, contained what was described as a copper breastplate and copper beads. A fragment of a textile was preserved under the copper.[268]

WELCOME MOUND (46MR003)

Several Adena mounds were on the property of the Columbia-Southern Chemical Corporation plant near New Martinsville, West Virginia, including the Natrium Mound and the Welcome Mound. In 1956, the chemical company had plans to expand its facility in the area of the mounds. Members of the WVAS, learning of the proposed expansion and impending destruction of the mounds, contacted the Columbia-Southern Chemical Corporation with their concerns. The chemical company agreed to fund an excavation of the mounds, and the Smithsonian Institution was contacted for assistance with the excavations. As a result, Frank M. Setzler, head curator of the Department of Anthropology of the Smithsonian, directed the excavations.[269]

Stone Shoveler Duck tubular effigy pipe from the Welcome Mound. *(Catalogue Mound No. A417000.0) Department of Anthropology, Smithsonian Institution.*

The Welcome Mound was approximately 110 feet in diameter and 14 feet at the highest point at the time of excavation. The mound fill was composed of topsoil, humus and a loose gravelly soil containing many waterworn pebbles from small to several inches across. The fill composition was like that of the nearby Natrium Mound and was difficult to shovel and trowel.[270]

The remains of three adult individuals were found in the Welcome Mound. Two of the three were placed near the center of the mound. The remains were badly decomposed and were covered and surrounded by "channels and molds, caused by decayed logs lying in various directions."[271]

Within a few feet of the individuals was a mass of broken sherds of coarse grit-tempered pottery vessels and some freshwater mussels. Setzler was able to reconstruct a very large pot from the sherds. The vessel was over one foot tall and barrel shaped with no constricted neck and a flat, undecorated rim. The outside surface treatment appeared to be smoothed over cordmarking.[272]

In the mouth of one of the individuals was the canine tooth of a mountain lion or cougar (*Felis concolor*). This was thought to indicate that the individual might have been a shaman or medicine man for the tribe.[273]

One of the most unusual finds from the excavation was a very finely made tubular stone effigy pipe in the shape of a Shoveler duck *Spatula clypeata*. The pipe was made from Ohio limestone and was found approximately five inches from the right knee of Burial No. 1 and six feet beneath the top of the mound.[274]

Pieces of charcoal from the base of the mound were radiocarbon tested by Michigan-Memorial Phoenix Project No. 6. Dr. James B. Griffin of the University of Michigan stated the results of the sample were 2300 ± 200 years, or around 341 BC.[275]

WILLOW ISLAND MOUND (46PL003)

The Willow Island Mound was located on Willow Island Bottom along the Ohio River in Pleasants County, West Virginia. Willow Island Bottom is an area approximately six miles long on the left bank of the Ohio River. The mound was on property owned by the Hammett family, who protected it for many years.[276] Sometime before 1978, the property was acquired by the Monongahela Power Company, which erected the Willow Island Power Station there. The nearby mound was protected by a chain-link fence.[277]

Eventually, with the threat of more development, scientific excavation of the mound was planned. Monongahela Power Company contracted with the West Virginia Geological and Economic Survey to conduct the excavations. The excavation took place over a three-month period in 1976. Monongahela Power Company provided support throughout the project. Now totally excavated, the Willow Island Mound was one of the few Adena mounds in West Virginia that was excavated by trained professional archaeologists at the time.

The Willow Island Mound was included in the Little Kanawha–Muskingham group of Adena mounds by McMichael.[278] It was thought to represent Adena mortuary activity in the area around the middle of the first millennium BC, or around 500 BC.[279]

The Willow Island excavations were significant in two respects. First, the excavation was conducted through a thorough hand excavation by a trained crew of archaeologists. Only a few earthen burial mounds in the Upper Ohio Valley had been scientifically investigated at the time, and that included the Natrium and Cresap Mounds in Marshall County, West Virginia.[280] Secondly, the Willow Island Mound was constructed around 500 BC, and the construction and use was rather simple compared to later Adena mortuary activity in that there was no significant reuse or disturbance after its completion.[281]

When excavations began in 1976, the mound was a "low symmetrical cone" with a 4-foot white oak tree growing on top. The mound was 8 feet high and 80 feet in diameter. A 10-foot grid system was used oriented to true north. The mound was stripped downward in arbitrary 1-foot levels. The area excavated included 5,600 square feet.[282]

Power equipment was used to remove the large tree stump on top of the mound and move the back dirt dumped at the outer edge of the mound and to scrape the sub-mound area when all other work was complete. Otherwise, excavation was done completely by hand. The mound fill from features and burials was screened through quarter-inch hardware cloth. Flotation was used to recover small organic remains.[283]

From variations in the color and texture in the mound fill soil, the excavators were able to distinguish between three distinct units: an Outer Mound, an Inner Mound and subsoil. Two radiocarbon dates were obtained for the mound from yellow pine charcoal. The date from the charcoal for the Inner Mound was 2405 ± 65 BP or 455 BC, and the date from wild cherry charcoal taken from the Outer Mound dated to 2285 ± 80 BP, or 315 BC.[284]

The excavation of the Willow Island Mound identified six human burials and fifteen features. Using several lines of evidence, the excavators were able to separate the burials and features into a "contemporary group" that represented Adena activity before or during the mound-building activity and an "intrusive group" referring to "prehistoric or historic activity after Adena abandonment."[285]

The contemporary group was further divided into (1) Adena activity on the mound site before mortuary or mound-building episodes, (2) the initial mortuary episode before mound building and (3) ritual activity during mound building.[286]

Features 1 and 13 and four post molds were included in the pre-mortuary activity period. These included a refuse pit in the subfloor and flint knapping debris in the subfloor.[287]

Burial 5, thought to be the principal burial, occurred during the initial mortuary activity period. The individual was buried in the subfloor a few feet north of the center of the mound. The burial contained the poorly preserved remains of an individual and a quadriconcave cannel shale gorget. Because of the dimensions of the grave, it was thought that the individual was buried in an extended position with his head toward the southwest.[288]

Within two feet of the principal burial was a cache of items (Feature 6) that included three Adena points, two cache blades, a hematite hemisphere, 1.4 kilograms of red ocher and a small cake of identified white powder. Charcoal fragments recovered from the feature included yellow pine, poplar and hickory.[289]

Feature 8 was a small oval pit at or near the center of the mound about 0.3 feet below floor level. It contained traces of red ocher. No other remains were found, or if present, they had completely disappeared.[290]

Feature 12 was a cache of copper beads and a bit of red ocher on the mound floor between the principal burial and a "grave post" structure (Feature 10). At least ninety-two copper beads were found in a "loosely coiled strand" on top of a small patch of fibrous organic material thought to be possibly bark. A few bits of yellow pine charcoal were also found.[291]

Feature 10 consisted of seven closely spaced post molds that appeared to be the remains of a rather complex post structure physically associated with Feature 12, the cache of copper beads. The post molds began at the mound floor level and extended into the subsoil. There was a heavy central post, about 1.1 feet in diameter, set vertically to a depth of 3.4 feet. Around this central post were six lighter posts arranged in a close ring.[292]

Feature 9 consisted of a small cache of objects on the mound floor halfway between Burials 5 and 6. The only remaining items were an Adena point, a patch of red ocher and mulberry charcoal fragments on top of an irregular organic stain about two square feet. This was thought to possibly have been the remains of a bark or woven container. There was evidence of a low earthen mound over the cache that consisted of an area of small organic stains in an oval approximately six and a half feet northeast to southwest and half a foot above the mound floor.[293]

Burial 6 was the second Adena burial interred in a subfloor pit near the southern edge of the Inner Mound. The grave was seven feet long and three feet wide in an irregular depression on the mound floor. The fill contained traces of refuse that included hickory charcoal, charred nutshell, an Adena pottery sherd and a piece of worked chert. The grave floor was flat with no lining. A cast of a small human skull was found. Within the cast were a trace of bone and small fragments of tooth enamel. The size and form of the remains suggested the burial of a small child or infant with his head to the southwest.[294]

Feature 5 was a cache of items near the center of the mound thought to have been deposited after the Inner Mound construction was taking place. Some of the items were about two and a half feet above the mound floor. The cache included an Adena point, a cache blade, a diorite celt and a strand of twenty-four copper beads. There was no evidence of a container. Yellow pine charcoal fragments were found among the cache items. There was some intrusion of oak roots.[295]

Feature 4 was a hearth covering an area about 6.0 feet long and 2.5 feet wide. A burned earth area approximately 0.3 feet above the mound floor was thought to be possibly contemporaneous with the deposition of the Inner Mound fill. In addition to burned earth, fire-cracked rock and wood charcoal were recovered.[296]

Features 14 and 15 consisted of two stone objects. Sometime during construction of the Outer Mound, a sandstone bowl and a large Adena point

Top: Stone bird effigy smoking pipe from the Willow Island Mound. *Courtesy of the Grave Creek Mound Archaeological Complex, West Virginia Department of Arts, Culture and History.*

Middle: Bifaces from the Willow Island Mound. *Courtesy of the Grave Creek Mound Archaeological Complex, West Virginia Department of Arts, Culture and History.*

Bottom: Adena groundstone mortuary items from the Willow Island Mound: A–C. Celts from Feature 6 and Inner Mound area; D. Shale gorget from Burial 5; E. Shale gorget from Outer Mound; F. Disc-shaped sandstone tablet from Outer Mound; G. Rectangular sandstone tablet from Burial 5; H and I. Grooved whetstones from the Outer Mound; J. Hematite hemisphere from Feature 5; K. Sandstone hemisphere from Outer Mound. *Courtesy of the Grave Creek Mound Archaeological Complex, West Virginia Department of Arts, Culture and History.*

Remains of intrusive historic horse burial in the Willow Island Mound. *Courtesy of the Grave Creek Mound Archaeological Complex, West Virginia Department of Arts, Culture and History.*

were intentionally broken and scattered. There were thirteen fragments of the sandstone bowl recovered 2.3 feet to 4.4 feet below the mound surface that appeared to be scattered from the mound center outward to the northeast. The large Adena point was recovered in five pieces.[297]

The Willow Island Mound was constructed over two Adena burials and associated mortuary items below the ground surface. One principal grave was lined with bark and held the remains of what was thought to be a young adult male. A unique post structure consisting of a yellow pine pole had been erected at the head of the grave. At some point during the mound-building sequence, the pole was burned and removed.[298] There were thought to have been two separate stages of mound construction over a short period of time.

Like many Ohio Valley mounds, the Willow Island Mound was used for additional burials. Four additional human burials were interred in the mound after the Adena occupation of the area. Two were adults, and one was an adolescent. The fourth burial consisted only of bone fragments. In addition, a later historic burial of a horse was found in the mound.[299]

Conclusion

Where do the people who built the mounds and earthworks in West Virginia fit into Ohio Valley history, and what do we know about them? Because of the excavations and studies conducted by archaeologists, there is a lot of information useful for addressing these questions, but it is also evident that there is still a lot to learn. What we do know is that for hundreds of generations spanning thousands of years, the Native American occupation of West Virginia was by small groups of mobile hunter-gatherers. This was the time before the construction of the mounds and earthworks discussed in the preceding chapter, when the material culture of the peoples living in the hills, hollows and valleys of the state was limited to a rather narrow assortment of primarily utilitarian tools/implements and personal items made of stone, bone, antler, wood, leather and fabric. At that time, local native peoples did not possess the technology to make ceramic pottery from local clays. Theirs was a mobile life in which they carried all their worldly goods as they moved their camp from location to location, which occurred frequently and often over rugged terrain. The archaeological evidence indicates that the day-to-day lives of the families who occupied these camps centered on domestic activities associated with the acquisition, processing and preparation of foods and the manufacture and repair of tools and other needed items. In other words, much of their time was probably spent making and acquiring the resources necessary to sustain themselves and their families. In West Virginia, evidence of houses or shelters is meager at best, and few burials are known. The burials that have been reported were placed in shallow graves within the camps with no or few adornments and little, if any, evidence of ceremony or ritual activity. The living quarters and burial areas were not clearly separated. Although styles of artifacts did change over time and some new technologies were introduced, the overall rate of culture change was slow.

In the upper and central Ohio Valley, this long-lived pattern gradually gave way to something new around 1200 to 1000 BC, generally corresponding to the beginning of the Woodland period. In general, the changes recognized by archaeologists at this time had their beginnings in the preceding Late Archaic and thus appear to represent a gradual in-place transition or evolution of beliefs, practices and technologies within local populations, rather than an abrupt or revolutionary change that might be expected by a rapid influx or migration of peoples from outside the area or region. At this time, the overall lifestyle of native peoples was not much different than it had been for the preceding millennia, although there was an increased reliance on domesticated plants, the use of ceramic pottery was more common and widespread and houses were more substantially constructed, perhaps reflecting a gradual shift toward a more sedentary way of life.

The archaeological evidence indicates that it was during this period that the first earthen mounds in the central and upper Ohio Valley were constructed and that nearly all of the mounds and earthworks were built within a span of approximately one millennium, from about 500 BC to AD 500. After this period, few mounds were constructed in the central and upper Ohio Valley. Ohio archaeologist Brad Lepper[300] notes that at the time of European arrival, there may have been up to ten thousand Native American mounds and earthworks in the Central Ohio Valley and that today about one thousand survive, with fewer than one hundred being open to the public. Marking cemeteries and other sacred places, these earthen constructions, some of which are of massive proportions, captured the imaginations of early European explorers, and where they are preserved and interpreted at state and federal parks and museums, they continue to attract thousands of visitors each year to witness their grandeur. In this region, archaeologists refer to the Early Woodland mounds and associated earthworks as Adena and those of the later Middle Woodland period as Hopewell. Both of these archaeological manifestations are known primarily from their mortuary customs and, to a lesser extent, from other aspects of their day-to-day lives. While Adena was a regional phenomenon located in areas of southern Ohio, eastern and central Kentucky, eastern Indiana and the Ohio River area of West Virginia, Hopewell influences spanned a much greater area extending from the Great Lakes region to Florida and from Kansas City to the Upper Ohio Valley, as evidenced by similar artifacts and mound and earthwork sites. The Hopewell trade network extended beyond this expanse, reaching as far as the Rocky Mountains in the west to the Atlantic Ocean in the east.[301]

Adena mounds were typically small conical constructions that covered one or more burials, with many being only a few to several feet in height. The first burial(s) was often placed in a pit or log-lined chamber or as a cremation below the original ground surface. While some burials were accompanied by offerings that included tubular pipes, shell beads, copper ornaments and skillfully crafted chipped-stone tools of high-quality flint, others lacked associated artifacts, demonstrating the high degree of variability in how the dead were treated. Because not all Adena peoples were buried in mounds, archaeologists believe that the individuals buried in them were somehow special—achieving some level of status or importance during life or in death. Once the burial and associated ceremonial activities were completed, the area was eventually covered with a layer of soil. Over time, subsequent burials were placed in some of the mounds, with additional layers of soil added to cover them. As new burials were added, the size of the mound grew, with some reaching impressive heights. The construction of Grave Creek Mound in West Virginia, which has a height of approximately seventy feet, represents multiple generations of construction and use.

Even though Adena mounds such as the Grave Creek Mound are impressive constructions, it is the large and imposing mound and earthworks complexes of the Middle Woodland Hopewell peoples that have most captured the imaginations and interests of archaeologists and the public. Most of the large Hopewell mound and earthwork sites are situated in south central Ohio on the boundary between the flat, glaciated country to the north and the unglaciated hill country to the south. The high degree of ecological diversity offered by these landscapes provided the inhabitants with a rich array of natural resources.

The focal area of Hopewell development was in the vicinity of Chillicothe in Ross County, Ohio, where mounds and earthworks of the Mound City Group, Hopeton Earthworks, High Bank Works, Hopewell Mound Group and Seip Earthworks are located in the valleys of the Scioto River and Paint Creek, a major tributary of the Scioto. Conical mounds like those of Adena are present, but so, too, are large loaf-shaped mounds and a variety of geometric earthworks in the form of circles, squares, rectangles and rarely other forms, including octagons. These and other sites located in adjacent river valleys, such as the Newark Earthworks located approximately sixty miles to the east on the South Fork of Licking River, are owned by the National Park Service, with the grounds containing hundreds of mounds and earthworks being open to the public. Some archaeologists believe that these large mound and earthwork sites served as ceremonial centers for multiple surrounding villages. Unlike Ohio, few archaeological parks and museums are located in West Virginia. The only one that combines a park and museum for Native American cultures is the state-owned and operated Grave Mound Archaeological Complex, which includes the Delf Norona Museum, located on the Ohio River in Moundsville.

In West Virginia, the largest concentrations of mounds and earthworks were located in the Greater Charleston area of the Kanawha Valley and in the Northern Panhandle region. The mounds in these areas, and West Virginia in general, have not been as extensively studied and reported as those in Ohio and Kentucky, and as noted previously, many of the excavations were conducted in the nineteenth century before modern techniques of excavation and analysis had been developed. As a consequence, much of the information currently available is lacking in detail and suffers from too few radiocarbon dates.

Some of these mounds and earthworks have been attributed to the Adena, the Hopewell and a mixture of both Adena and Hopewell influences. For the large complex of mounds and earthworks near Charleston, McMichael and Mairs[302] suggested that the apparent flurry of construction during what is typically considered the Middle Woodland temporal period was influenced, directly or indirectly, by Hopewellian societies, presumably from Ohio. However, other archaeologists saw the mounds and associated mortuary activities as an in-place development of outside influences on a local base culture.[303] Wilkins's interpretation appears to more accurately support the current archaeological record, as there is little evidence for a Hopewell presence in the Kanawha Valley or West Virginia in general.

It is evident that much remains to be learned about the origins of mound building in West Virginia and the identities of the native peoples who constructed the mounds. This will require the reanalysis of existing collections and data and new excavations focused on local sites dating from around 2000 BC to AD 500. While the mound-building cultures in the Kanawha Valley and Northern Panhandle each constructed mounds and earthworks, each likely developed from a different base culture and had its own unique developmental history. Therefore, it is perhaps best to not view West Virginia mounds and earthworks as Adena or Hopewell but rather as local expressions of a geographically broad mortuary program that included the construction of mounds and earthworks and complex ceremonial behaviors, within which a number of related but distinct societies participated.

GLOSSARY OF ARCHAEOLOGICAL TERMS

appendage: An addition to the main body, such as on a pottery vessel. Strap handles and lugs are appendages.

applied rim strip: A strip of clay sometimes found on prehistoric pottery applied around the neck of the vessel.

artifact: An object made or used by a particular group of people or culture.

ascribed status: A social rank that is assigned at birth or later in life, as opposed to achieved status (which is earned).

assemblage: A group of artifacts found together that are thought to have been used by the same group of people.

beamer: A bone tool used for scraping animal hides.

biface: A stone tool or projectile point that has been worked on both sides.

calcined bone: A bone that has been burned and is white in color.

castellations: A series of vertical appendages around the top of a pottery rim.

celt: A long ground or flaked tool similar to an axe or adze, probably attached to a wooden handle.

chronology: A series of events arranged in the order in which they occurred.

component: An occupation by a specific culture or at a specific time.

conchoidal fracture: Breaking in a curved, semicircular pattern similar to ripples in a mussel or marine shell. This usually occurs in fine-grained minerals, such as obsidian, chert (flint) and sometimes quartz.

culture: A collection of customs, language, beliefs and materials shared by a specific society; a specific group of people with shared customs, language and beliefs.

debitage: Waste material left behind from the manufacture of stone tools.

faunal: Pertaining to animals.

feature: Archaeological evidence in the ground that cannot be removed; examples: post molds, fire hearths, storage pits.

floral: Pertaining to plants.

habitation: A place of residence.

in situ: In its original place; not out of context.

lithics: Items and tools made from stone.

mammiform: Shaped like a breast.

material culture: Tangible artifacts left by a specific group of people.

midden: An area in a village where trash was deposited.

mortuary: Relating to burials or tombs.

multicomponent: An archaeological site that has more than one occupation over time.

ovoid: Shaped like an egg.

paleoethnobotany: The analysis of prehistoric plant remains.

phases of excavation: Guidelines developed under Section 106 of the National Historic Preservation Act of 1966. These phases apply to all archaeological projects in the United States with federal involvement or federal funding. 1) Phase I (identification): to determine if an archaeological site is present; 2) Phase II (evaluation): to determine the importance of the site and if more work or total excavation is warranted; and 3) Phase III (mitigation/ data recovery); total excavation of the site, analysis of artifacts recovered and production of a technical report.

plow zone: The top layer of soil from the surface to the depth a plow might penetrate archaeological deposits.

post mold or posthole: A dark circular stain in the soil left behind after a wooden post, usually from a house or palisade wall, has decayed.

provenience: The exact location of an artifact or deposit on a site.

punctates: Decorations, usually on pottery, made of circular indentations formed with a round stick pressed into clay before the vessel is fired.

saltpan: A shallow pottery vessel used for gathering salt from evaporated salt brine.

sherd: A piece of broken pottery.

stratigraphy: The layers of deposits at an archaeological site.

surface treatment: A way of roughing up the surface of a pottery vessel before firing to keep it from slipping when wet. Prehistoric potters used a variety of surface treatments, such as a cordwrapped paddle, knotted net and even dried corncobs on the outer surface of the vessel.

temper: Material added to pottery before firing to keep it from shrinking or cracking when fired. Crushed rock and crushed mussel shell were common tempers.

uniface: A stone tool that is worked on only one side.

vasiform: Resembling a vessel or vase.

NOTES

Preface

1. Trader, "Mound Builders."

Chapter 1

2. Lepper, *Ohio Archaeology*, 82.
3. Broyles, "Preliminary Report," 1–43; Broyles, "Second Preliminary Report."

Chapter 2

4. Applegate, "Woodland Taxonomy," 13; Pacheco and Burks, "Early Woodland Ceremonialism," 175.
5. Clay, "Adena Ritual Spaces"; Seeman, "Adena 'Houses.'"
6. Seeman, "Adena 'Houses'"; Pecora and Burks, "Bremen Site."
7. Pacheco and Burks, "Early Woodland Ceremonialism," 181.
8. Lepper, *Ohio Archaeology*, 82.
9. Ibid., 83.
10. Maslowski, "Introduction to West Virginia Pottery Types," 4.

11. Pacheco, "Woodland Period Archaeology"; Pecora and Burks, "Bremen Site"; Pullins et al., Contract Publication Series; Seeman, "Adena 'Houses.'"
12. Schweikart, "Upland Settlement in the Adena Heartland."
13. Lepper, *Ohio Archaeology*, 81.
14. Seeman, *Hopewell Interaction Sphere.*
15. Thomas, *Report on the Mound Explorations*, 414.

Chapter 3

16. Hemmings, "Investigations at Grave Creek Mound," 5.
17. Farnsworth and Emerson, "Early Woodland Archeology," 566.
18. Seeman, "Adena 'Houses.'"
19. Lepper, *Ohio Archaeology*, 105.
20. Maslowski, "Introduction to West Virginia Pottery Types," 4.
21. Rafferty and Mann, *Smoking and Culture.*
22. Ibid., ix.
23. Ibid., xii.
24. Ibid., xii.
25. Norona, "Grave Creek 'Shepherd' Tablet."

Chapter 4

26. Smith, Introduction, *Report on the Mound Explorations*, 5.
27. Thomas, *Report on the Mound Explorations*, 21.
28. Smith, Introduction, *Report on the Mound Explorations*, 9.
29. Ibid.
30. Ibid., 10.
31. Ibid., 14.
32. Ibid., 15.

Chapter 5

33. Bache and Satterthwaite, "Excavations of an Indian Mound," 133.
34. Ibid., 156.
35. Ibid., 134.

NOTES TO PAGES 39–53

37. Ibid.
38. Ibid., 136.
39. Ibid., 157.
40. Dragoo, "Mounds for the Dead," 147–49.
41. Ibid., 147.
42. Ibid.
43. Ibid., 147–48.
44. Ibid., 148.
45. Ibid.
46. Ibid., 150.
47. Ibid., 148.
48. Ibid., 149.
49. Ibid.
50. Woodward and McDonald, *Indian Mounds of the Middle Ohio Valley*, 275–76.
51. Ibid., 278.
52. Ibid., 276.
53. GAI Consultants, *Executive Summary*, 2.
54. Ibid.
55. Anslinger, "Cotiga Mound."
56. GAI Consultants, *Executive Summary*, 2.
57. Ibid., 1.
58. Anslinger, "Cotiga Mound."
59. Frankenberg and Henning, *Phase III Data Recovery*, iv.
60. Ibid.
61. Ibid.
62. Ibid.
63. Ibid.
64. Ibid.
65. Ibid., 273.
66. Ibid., 295
67. Ibid., iv.
68. Anslinger, "Cotiga Mound."
69. Ibid.
70. Ibid.
71. Dragoo, "Mounds for the Dead," 9.
72. Ibid., 7.
73. Ibid.

74. Ibid., 8.
75. Ibid.
76. Ibid., 9.
77. Ibid., 11.
78. Ibid., 12.
79. Ibid., 13.
80. Ibid.
81. Ibid., 14–18.
82. Ibid., 18.
83. Ibid., 19.
84. Ibid.
85. Dragoo, "Cresap Mound," 4.
86. Dragoo, "Mounds for the Dead," 22.
87. Ibid., 72.
88. Ibid., 73.
89. Sutton, "Doddridge County Mounds," 23.
90. Ibid.
91. Ibid., 24.
92. Ibid.
93. Ibid.
94. Ibid., 25.
95. Ibid., 26.
96. Ibid.
97. Ibid.
98. Ibid., 27.
99. Hemmings, "Fairchance Site," 46.
100. Hemmings, "Fairchance Mound," 3.
101. Ibid., 4.
102. Ibid., 10.
103. Ibid.
104. Ibid.
105. Ibid., 21.
106. Hemmings, "Fairchance Site," 49.
107. Ibid.
108. Ibid., 51.
109. Hemmings, "Fairchance Mound," 65–67.
110. Ibid., 12.
111. Ibid., 60.

112. Ibid., 63.
113. Ibid.
114. Ibid., 60.
115. McMichael and Mairs, "Salvage Excavation," 23.
116. Hemmings, "Fairchance Mound," 58.
117. Ibid., 52.
118. Ibid.
119. Wilkins, "Salvage Excavations," 1.
120. Ibid., 10.
121. Ibid., 1.
122. Ibid.
123. Ibid.
124. Ibid., 5.
125. Ibid.
126. Ibid.
127. Ibid., 7.
128. Ibid., 8.
129. Trader, "Grave Creek Mound."
130. Norona, *Moundsville's Mammoth Mound*, 15.
131. Hemmings, "Investigations at Grave Creek Mound," 5.
132. Norona, *Moundsville's Mammoth Mound*, 11.
133. Ibid.
134. Ibid.
135. Quaife, "Journals of Captain Meriwether Lewis," 41.
136. Norona, *Moundsville's Mammoth Mound*, 11.
137. Ibid.
138. Ibid., 12.
139. Ibid., 11.
140. Hemmings, "Investigations at Grave Creek Mound," 10.
141. Ibid.
142. Norona, "Grave Creek 'Shepherd' Tablet."
143. Hemmings, "Investigations at Grave Creek Mound," 10.
144. Ibid.
145. Norona, *Moundsville's Mammoth Mound*, 15.
146. Ibid., 15–16.
147. Ibid., 17.
148. Ibid.
149. Ibid., 15.
150. Ibid., 17.

151. Ibid., 18.
152. Ibid., 18–19.
153. Ibid., 19.
154. Ibid., 22.
155. Ibid.
156. Ibid., 23.
157. Ibid.
158. Ibid., 24.
159. Ibid., 25.
160. Ibid., 26.
161. Ibid., 27.
162. Ibid., 28.
163. Webb and Snow, *Adena People*, 8.
164. Norona, *Moundsville's Mammoth Mound*, 31.
165. Ibid., 32.
166. Ibid., 33.
167. Ibid., 34.
168. Ibid., 35.
169. Ibid., 43.
170. Ibid.
171. Ibid., 44.
172. Ibid., 48.
173. Ibid.
174. Ibid., 48–49.
175. Ibid., 33.
176. Ibid., 50.
177. Trader, "Grave Creek Mound."
178. Quaife, "Journals of Captain Meriwether Lewis."
179. Fowler et al., "Some Recent Additions to Adena Archeology."
180. Hemmings, "Investigations at Grave Creek Mound," 3.
181. Ibid.
182. Ibid.
183. Ibid.
184. Norona, *Moundsville's Mammoth Mound*, 38.
185. Ibid., 37.
186. Ibid., 36–42.
187. Dragoo, "Mounds for the Dead," 151.
188. Fetzer and Mayer-Oakes, "Excavation of an Adena Burial Mound," 5.
189. Dragoo, "Mounds for the Dead," 152.

190. Ibid.

191. Fetzer, "Notes on Mound No. 3," 8.

192. Ibid.

193. Ibid., 9.

194. Dragoo, "Mounds for the Dead," 152; Mayer-Oakes, "Prehistory of the Upper Ohio Valley," 184.

195. Broyles, "Mounds in Randolph County," 9.

196. Ibid.

197. Woodward and McDonald, *Indian Mounds of the Middle Ohio Valley*, 273.

198. Ibid.

199. Thomas, *Report on the Mound Explorations*, 414.

200. Ibid.

201. Norris, Huddleson's enclosure.

202. Thomas, *Report on the Mound Explorations*, 416.

203. Ibid., 417.

204. Ibid.

205. Ibid.

206. Ibid., 418.

207. Ibid.

208. Youse, "Excavation of the Young Mound," 21–29.

209. Thomas, *Report on the Mound Explorations*, 425.

210. Ibid.

211. Ibid., 426.

212. Ibid.

213. Ibid., 427.

214. Ibid., 428.

215. Norris, Huddleson's enclosure.

216. Thomas, *Report on the Mound Explorations*, 428.

217. Ibid.

218. Ibid.

219. Ibid.

220. Ibid., 429.

221. Ibid., 430.

222. Youse, "Excavation of the Young Mound," 5.

223. Thomas, *Report on the Mound Explorations*, 431.

224. Ibid.

225. Youse, "Excavation of the Young Mound," 7.

226. Ibid., 8.

227. Ibid., 18.
228. Maslowski et al., "The Kentucky, Ohio and West Virginia Radiocarbon Database."
229. Thomas, *Report on the Mound Explorations*, 432.
230. Ibid.
231. Ibid.
232. Ibid.
233. Ibid.
234. McMichael and Mairs, "Salvage Excavation," 23.
235. Ibid.
236. Ibid.
237. Ibid., 25.
238. Ibid.
239. Ibid., 25–26.
240. Ibid., 26.
241. Ibid.
242. Ibid., 26–31.
243. Ibid., 31.
244. Ibid., 32.
245. Hemmings, "West Virginia Radiocarbon Dates," 38–39.
246. McMichael and Mairs, "Excavation of the Murad Mound," 1.
247. Ibid., 2.
248. Ibid., 5.
249. Ibid., 7.
250. Ibid.
251. Ibid., 9.
252. Ibid., 7.
253. Ibid., 9.
254. Ibid., 12
255. Ibid., 13–14.
256. Anderson, *Human Skeleton*, 127.
257. Ibid., 15.
258. Ibid., 18.
259. Dragoo, "Mounds for the Dead," 318.
260. Ibid., 319.
261. Ibid., 317–18.
262. Ibid., 318.
263. Ibid., 322.

264. Ibid.
265. Ibid., 142.
266. Ibid., 142; Solecki, "Exploration of an Adena Mound at Natrium," 317.
267. Dragoo, "Mounds for the Dead," 142.
268. Solecki, "Exploration of an Adena Mound at Natrium," 353.
269. Setzler, "Welcome Mound," 4.
270. Ibid., 5.
271. Ibid., 6.
272. Ibid.
273. Ibid.
274. Ibid., 11.
275. Ibid., 6.
276. Hemmings, "Exploration of an Early Adena Mound at Willow Island," iii.
277. Ibid.
278. McMichael, "Adena-East."
279. Hemmings, "Exploration of an Early Adena Mound at Willow Island," 1.
280. Solecki, "Exploration of an Adena Mound at Natrium"; Dragoo, "Mounds for the Dead."
281. Hemmings, "Exploration of an Early Adena Mound at Willow Island," 3.
282. Ibid., 6.
283. Ibid., 7.
284. Ibid., 12.
285. Ibid.
286. Ibid.
287. Ibid., 15.
288. Ibid., 16.
289. Ibid.
290. Ibid., 18.
291. Ibid.
292. Ibid., 18–19.
293. Ibid., 19.
294. Ibid., 19–20.
295. Ibid., 21.
296. Ibid.
297. Ibid.
298. Ibid., 1.

299. Ibid., 24.
300. Lepper, *Ohio Archaeology*, 94.
301. Seeman, *Hopewell Interaction Sphere*.
302. McMichael and Mairs, "Excavation of the Murad Mound."
303. Wilkins, "Kanawha Tradition," 63–81.

BIBLIOGRAPHY

Anderson, James E. *The Human Skeleton: A Manual for Archaeologists.* Ottawa: National Museum of Canada, Department of Northern Affairs and Natural Resources, 1962.

Anslinger, C. Michael. "Cotiga Mound." e-WV: The West Virginia Encyclopedia. February 8, 2011. www.wvencyclopedia.org/articles/1609.

Applegate, Darlene. "Woodland Taxonomy in the Middle Ohio Valley: A Historical Overview." *Woodland Period Systematics in the Middle Ohio Valley.* Tuscaloosa: University of Alabama Press, 2005, 1–18.

Bache, Charles, and Linton Satterthwaite Jr. "Excavations of an Indian Mound at Beech Bottom." *The Museum Journal* 3–4 (September–December 1930): 133–63. Museum of the University of Pennsylvania–Philadelphia.

Broyles, Bettye J. "Mounds in Randolph County." *Eastern States Archeological Federation Bulletin* 23, no. 9 (1964).

———. "Preliminary Report: The St. Albans Site (46 Ka 27), Kanawha County, West Virginia." *West Virginia Archeologist* 19 (1966): 1–43

———. "Second Preliminary Report: The St. Albans Site (46 Ka 27), Kanawha County, West Virginia." *Report of Archeological Investigations* 3, West Virginia Geological and Economic Survey, Morgantown, WV.

Clay, R. Berle. "Adena Ritual Spaces." *Early Woodland Archeology* (1986): 581–95.

Clay, R. Berle, and Charles M. Niquette. *Middle Woodland Mortuary Ritual in the Gallipolis Locks and Dam Vicinity, Mason County, West Virginia.* 1992.

Dragoo, Don W. "Cresap Mound (46Mr7) Preliminary Report." *West Virginia Archeologist* 11 (1959).

———. "Mounds for the Dead: An Analysis of the Adena Culture." *Annals of the Carnegie Museum* 37 (1963). Pittsburgh, Pennsylvania.

Farnsworth, Kenneth B., and Thomas E. Emerson. "Early Woodland Archeology." Center for American Archeology, *Kampsville Seminars in Archeology* 2 (1986).

Fetzer, E.W. "Notes on Mound No. 3 at the Half-Moon Site." *West Virginia Archeologist* 10 (1958): 7–9.

Fetzer, E.W., and William J. Mayer-Oakes. "Excavation of an Adena Burial Mound at the Half-Moon Site." *West Virginia Archeologist* 4 (1951): 1–25.

Fowler, Daniel B., E. Thomas Hemmings and Gary R. Wilkins. "Some Recent Additions to Adena Archeology in West Virginia." *Archaeology of Eastern North America* 4 (1976): 110–21.

Frankenberg, Susan R., and Grace E. Henning. *Phase III Data Recovery Investigations of the Cotiga Mound (46MO1), Mingo County, West Virginia.* West Virginia Department of Transportation Division of Highways, Charleston, West Virginia. Project 90-509-12 (1994).

GAI Consultants. *Executive Summary: The Cotiga Mound Archaeological Excavation: Appalachian Corridor G.* (1993).

Haag, William G. "The Pottery from the Morgan Stone Site." In *The Morgan Mound* by William S. Webb. University of Kentucky Reports in Anthropology and Archaeology 5, no. 3 (1941): 263–67.

Hemmings, E. Thomas. "The Core Drilling Project at Grave Creek Mound: Preliminary Results and Radiocarbon Date." *West Virginia Archeologist* 26 (1977): 59–68.

———. "Exploration of an Early Adena Mound at Willow Island, West Virginia." *West Virginia Geological and Economic Survey Report of Archeological Investigations* 7 (1978).

———. "Fairchance Mound and Village: An Early Middle Woodland Settlement in the Upper Ohio Valley." *West Virginia Archeologist* 36, no. 1 (1984a): 3–68.

———. "The Fairchance Site: Middle Woodland Settlement and Subsistence in the Upper Ohio Valley." *West Virginia Archeologist* 26 (1977): 46–58.

———. "Investigations at Grave Creek Mound 1975–76: A Sequence for Mound and Moat Construction." *West Virginia Archeologist* 36, no. 2 (1984b): 3–49.

———. "West Virginia Radiocarbon Dates and Prehistory." *West Virginia Archeologist* 37, no. 2 (1985): 35–43.

Lepper, Bradley T. *Ohio Archaeology: An Illustrated Chronicle of Ohio's Ancient American Cultures.* Wilmington, OH: Orange Frazier Press, 2005.

Maslowski, Robert F. "Introduction to West Virginia Pottery Types." Workshop presented at the Annual Meeting of the West Virginia Archeological Society, Parkersburg, West Virginia, 1982.

Maslowski, Robert F., C.M. Niquette and D.M. Wingfield. "The Kentucky, Ohio and West Virginia Radiocarbon Database." *West Virginia Archeologist* 47, nos. 1–2 (1995).

Mayer-Oakes, William J. "Prehistory of the Upper Ohio Valley: An Introductory Archeological Study." (Anthropological Series No. 2). *Annals of the Carnegie Museum* 34 (1955).

McMichael, Edward V. "Adena-East, an Appraisal of the More Easterly Extensions of the Spread of the Adena Phenomenon." In *Adena: The Seeking of an Identity. A Symposium Held at the Kitselman Conference Center*, edited by B.K. Swartz Jr. Ball State University (1970): 88–99.

———. "Archeological Salvage and Analysis of Two Kanawha Valley Mounds (46Bo24 and 46Ka18)." *West Virginia Archeologist* 18 (1965): 31–44.

McMichael, Edward V., and Oscar L. Mairs. "Excavation of the Murad Mound, Kanawha County, West Virginia and an Analysis of Kanawha Valley Mounds." *West Virginia Geological and Economic Survey Report of Archeological Investigations*, no. 1 (1969).

———. "Salvage Excavation of the Leslie Mound (46PU3) Putnam County, West Virginia." *West Virginia Archeologist* 15 (1963): 23–40.

Norona, Delf. "Comments on Townsend's Account of the 1838 Excavation of the Grave Creek Mound." *West Virginia Archeologist* 14 (1962): 7–9.

———. "The Dimensions of Moundsville's Mammoth Mound." *West Virginia Archeologist* 10 (1958): 13–19.

———. "The Grave Creek 'Shepherd' Tablet." *West Virginia Archeologist* 2, nos. 4–6 (1950a).

———. "The Lakin Tablet." *West Virginia Archeologist* 2 (1950b).

———. *Moundsville's Mammoth Mound*. West Virginia Archeological Society, 2008. Repr.

Norris, P.W. Huddleson's enclosure. Fayette County, Box 7, MS 2400, Division of Mound Exploration Records, National Anthropological Archives, Smithsonian Institution.

Pacheco, Paul J. "Woodland Period Archaeology in Central Ohio." *Ohio Archaeological Council Newsletter* 3, no. 3 (1991): 4–9.

Pacheco, Paul J., and Jarrod Burks. "Chapter 7: Early Woodland Ceremonialism in Context: Results of LCALS, Research at the Munson Springs Site (33LI251)." In *Transitions: Archaic and Early Woodland Research in the Ohio County*, edited by Marth P. Otto and Brian G. Redmond. Athens: Ohio University Press, 2008.

Pecora, Albert M., and Jarrod Burks. "The Bremen Site: A Terminal Late Archaic Period Upland Occupation in Fairfield County, Ohio." *The Emergence of the Moundbuilders: The Archaeology of Tribal Societies in Southeastern Ohio.* Athens: Ohio University Press, 2014.

Pullins, Stevan C., C. Michael Anslinger, Andrew Bradbury, Alexandra Bybee, Flora Church, Darla Spencer and William D. Updike. Cultural Resource Analysts, Inc., Contract Publication Series WV08-22, (2008) Hurricane, WV.

Quaife, M.M., ed. "The Journals of Captain Meriwether Lewis and Sergeant John Ordway Kept on the Expedition of Western Exploration, 1803–1806." *Publication of the State Historical Society of Wisconsin* 22 (1916): 41.

Rafferty, Sean M., and Rob Mann. *Smoking and Culture: The Archaeology of Tobacco Pipes in Eastern North America.* Knoxville: University of Tennessee Press, 2004.

Sassaman, Kenneth E. *Early Pottery in the Southeast: Tradition and Innovation in Cooking Technology.* Tuscaloosa: University of Alabama Press, 1993.

Schweikart, John F. "Upland Settlement in the Adena Heartland: Preliminary Evidence and Interpretations from Two Early Woodland Nonmortuary Habitations in Perry County, Ohio." In *Transitions: Archaic and Early Woodland Research in the Ohio Country*, edited by Marth P. Otto and Brian G. Redmond. Athens: Ohio University Press, 2008.

Seeman, Mark F. "Adena 'Houses' and Their Implications for Early Woodland Settlement Models in the Ohio Valley." *Early Woodland Archeology* (1986): 564–80.

———. *The Hopewell Interaction Sphere: The Evidence for Interregional Trade and Structural Complexity.* N.p.: Indiana Historical Society, 1979.

Setzler, Frank M. "Welcome Mound and the Effigy Pipes of the Adena People." *West Virginia Archeologist* 12 (1960): 4–14.

Smith, Bruce D. Introduction to the 1985 Edition. *Report on the Mound Explorations of the Bureau of Ethnology* by Cyrus Thomas. Washington, D.C.: Smithsonian Institution Press, 1894.

Solecki, Ralph S. "Exploration of an Adena Mound at Natrium, West Virginia." *Anthropological Papers* 40. *Smithsonian Institution Bureau of Ethnology Bulletin* 151 (1953): 313–96.

Squier, Ephraim, and Edwin Davis. *Ancient Monuments of the Mississippi Valley: Comprising the Results of Extensive Original Surveys and Explorations.*

Smithsonian Institution's Contribution to Knowledge Series. Washington, D.C.: Smithsonian Institution, 1848.

Sutton, Ernest R. "Doddridge County Mounds Nos. 46Do-1 to 46Do-5: Description of the Location, Excavation Work, and the Discoveries at a Group of Mounds in the Vicinity of Morgansville and Blandville, Doddridge County, West Va." *West Virginia Archeologist* 10 (1958): 23–27.

Thomas, Cyrus. *Report on the Mound Explorations of the Bureau of Ethnology.* Introduction by Bruce D. Smith. Washington, D.C.: Smithsonian Institution Press, 1894.

Townsend, Thomas. "Grave Creek Mound." (Reproduced verbatim from the *Cincinnati Chronicle* 3, no. 18, February 2, 1839, whole No. 122, E.D. Mansfield, editor). *West Virginia Archeologist* 14 (1962): 10–18.

Trader, Patrick D. "Grave Creek Mound." e-WV: The West Virginia Encyclopedia. September 27, 2013. www.wvencyclopedia.org/articles/2150.

———. "Mound Builders." e-WV: The West Virginia Encyclopedia. April 17, 2017. www.wvencyclopedi.org/articles/1424.

Webb, William S. "Engraved Tablets in the Wright Mounds: Sites 6 and 7 Montgomery County, Kentucky." *University of Kentucky Reports in Anthropology* 5, no. 1 (1940).

Webb, William S., and Charles E. Snow. *The Adena People.* 1945. Repr., Knoxville: University of Tennessee Press, 1974.

Wilkins, Gary R. "The Kanawha Tradition: A Review and Re-evaluation." *Tennessee Anthropologist* 4, no. 1 (1979): 63–81.

———. "Salvage Excavations of the Gore Mound (46 Bo 26)." *West Virginia Archeologist* 26 (1977): 1–12.

Woodward, Susan L., and Jerry N. McDonald. *Indian Mounds of the Middle Ohio Valley: A Guide to Mounds and Earthworks of the Adena, Hopewell, Cole, and Fort Ancient People.* Blacksburg, VA: McDonald and Woodward Publishing Company, 2002.

Youse, Hillis J. "Excavation of the Young Mound and Identification of Other Mounds in Dunbar, West Virginia." *West Virginia Archeologist* 22 (1969): 4–27.

INDEX

ABOUT THE AUTHOR

Darla Spencer is a registered professional archaeologist (RPA). She is currently a board of directors member of the Council for West Virginia Archaeology. She has been published in the *West Virginia Archeologist* and the *Quarterly Bulletin of the Archaeological Society of Virginia* and wrote several entries on West Virginia prehistory for the *West Virginia Encyclopedia* (2006). In 2002, she was awarded the Sigfus Olafson Award of Merit from the WVAS for contributions to the archaeology of West Virginia. Her first book, *Early Native Americans in West Virginia: The Fort Ancient Culture*, was published in 2016.

Visit us at
www.historypress.com
....